An Introduction to
Critical Reading

SEVENTH EDITION

LEAH McCRANEY

University of Alabama at Birmingham

WADSWORTH
CENGAGE Learning

Australia • Brazil • Japan • Korea • Mexico • Singapore • Spain • United Kingdom • United States

WADSWORTH
CENGAGE Learning

An Introduction to Critical Reading, Seventh Edition

Leah McCraney

Publisher: Lyn Uhl

Director of Developmental English: Annie Todd

Development Editor: Margaret Manos

Assistant Editor: Melanie Opacki

Editorial Assistant: Matt Conte

Media Editor: Amy Gibbons

Marketing Manager: Kirsten Stoller

Marketing Coordinator: Ryan Ahern

Marketing Communications Manager: Stacey Purviance

Content Project Manager: Dan Saabye

Art Director: Jill Ort

Print Buyer: Sue Spencer

Rights Acquisition Specialist, Image: Jennifer Meyer Dare

Rights Acquisition Specialist, Text: Katie Huha

Production Service: MPS Limited, a Macmillan Company

Cover Designer: Althea Chen

Cover Image: Superstock

Compositor: MPS Limited, a Macmillan Company

For product information and technology assistance, contact us at
Cengage Learning Customer & Sales Support, 1-800-354-9706
For permission to use material from this text or product,
submit all requests online at **www.cengage.com/permissions.**
Further permissions questions can be emailed to
permissionrequest@cengage.com.

Library of Congress Control Number: 2010934397

Student Edition:
ISBN-13: 978-0-495-80179-5
ISBN-10: 0-495-80179-8

Wadsworth
20 Channel Center Street
Boston, MA 02210
USA

Cengage Learning is a leading provider of customized learning solutions with office locations around the globe, including Singapore, the United Kingdom, Australia, Mexico, Brazil and Japan. Locate your local office at **international.cengage.com/region**

Cengage Learning products are represented in Canada by Nelson Education, Ltd.

For your course and learning solutions, visit **www.cengage.com.**

Purchase any of our products at your local college store or at our preferred online store **www.cengagebrain.com. Instructors:** Please visit **login.cengage.com** and log in to access instructor-specific resources.

Printed in the United States of America
2 3 4 5 6 7 15 14 13 12

In Memory of

Randy Marsh

Deep in December, it's nice to remember,
Without a hurt the heart is hollow.
Deep in December, it's nice to remember,
The fire of September that made us mellow.
Deep in December, our hearts should remember
And follow.

−The Fantasticks

Preface

New to the 7th Edition

- Seven new poems, including selections by Julia Alvarez, Billy Collins, Sekou Sundiata, e.e. cummings, William Stafford, Yusef Komunyakaa, and Ai.
- Three new short stories by Chimamanda Ngozi Adichie, Tobias Wolff, and Judy Budnitz.
- Eight new essays, by authors Kate Schmidt, William J. Chambliss, Cindy Ross Scope, Nicholas Bramble, Doug Fodeman and Marje Monroe, Larry Magid, Michael Dillingham, and Alton Fitzgerald White.
- A new textbook chapter on sociology.
- An updated Instructor's Manual to accompany the text.

To the Student

The readings in this book were selected for a number of reasons. First, they are all excellent pieces of writing. Second, they comprise a representative sample of four common types of writing: poetry, fiction, essays, and textbook chapters. Third, they are thought provoking.

This third reason is of utmost importance to the purposes of this book. Meaningful learning occurs when one is actively involved in the learning process, when one finds something in the process that is of personal importance. The majority of readings in this book offer ideas that are likely to be important to most readers. Literature in particular offers a field of universal ideas—after all, the essence of literature is life—and this is one reason such a wide variety of literature has been included here.

Reading allows one the opportunity to examine one's own principles and the principles of others. The Socratic position is that the unexamined life is not worth living. This position suggests that one must value one's own thinking and judgment, and is grounded in the belief that examining—questioning—is the foundation for being free.

Preface
To the Instructor

An Introduction to Critical Reading is an anthology of poems, short stories, essays, and college textbook chapters. The Instructor's Manual that accompanies the anthology presents an approach to developmental reading that departs from the traditional, skills-based approach. The manual suggests ways of using the pieces in the anthology to improve reading skills and critical thinking. The anthology is different from other developmental reading texts in its rationale and in its content.

The pieces in the anthology were selected not on the basis of a "readability formula" but because they are representative of the materials college students are required to read and because they encourage critical thinking. The selections for each genre present a range of difficulties, permitting instructors to choose texts appropriate to the abilities of their specific classes. Texts containing extensive literary allusions or problems of style, such as stream of consciousness, are not included. Such pieces require more time than the primary purposes of a reading course allow.

The selections were made with critical thinking and critical reading in mind. A detailed discussion of critical thinking—a term that has a variety of meanings—is included in the introductory essay of the Instructor's Manual. Suffice it to say that the heart of critical thinking is an active, personal involvement stemming from a desire "to know." Students who become actively involved in a text will eventually come to terms with it. This does not mean students will understand all of the information contained in a piece or make every possible inference. But most college students, regardless of their developmental status, can discern the essential message of a piece if they want "to know." The pieces in the anthology revolve around issues that are of interest to most readers: family, relationships, society, and so forth. The selections also reflect the cultural diversity of college readers. Over half of the selections are by women and nonwhite writers.

To eliminate some problems of comprehension and to provide the best possible opportunity for active involvement, the anthology provides the following aids:

1. Definitions of difficult words that are not defined in context.
2. Explanatory notes on allusions to literature, history, art, and so on.
3. A glossary that includes definitions and examples of common literary and rhetorical devices.

The anthology does not include questions on the content of the pieces. The Instructor's Manual discusses the importance of encouraging student questions and student-generated criteria. Questions that come from editors invite a mechanical investigation of what the editors think to be important. Such an investigation limits the possibilities of a piece of writing and limits student thinking to those points addressed by the questions. There is a need, of course, for some teacher questions and teacher-generated criteria. The Instructor's Manual provides such criteria, not only for evaluating the content of a piece, but also for developing critical thinking. The suggestions in the manual are not meant to limit the teacher's approach, but to suggest typical questions that can accomplish specific goals.

The critical thinking material is in the Instructor's Manual. None is included in the anthology for the following reasons:

1. Students tend either to ignore explanatory material or to embrace it so completely that they do not go beyond it and think independently.
2. Students become better readers by reading—not by being told how to read.
3. Textbook generalizations about how an adult *should* read, how *good* readers read, and what a reader *ought* to glean from a piece of writing exclude consideration of the great variety of effective reading styles and of the possible differences in readers' interpretations.
4. An instructor's ideas about the reading process or about a "good" college reader are far more suitable for that teacher's actual audience than a textbook apparatus written for an implied audience.

The Instructor's Manual contains the following:

1. An introductory essay that explains the rationale for the anthology, discusses the nature of critical thinking, and provides general guidelines for helping students develop critical thinking.
2. Articles for the instructor on attention deficit hyperactivity disorder and dyslexia.
3. A discussion of each selection in the anthology, explicating content and pointing out issues that teachers may want to explore in class discussions.
4. Specific suggestions for each piece contained in the anthology. These suggestions are intended to involve students in the content of the piece and to encourage the development of critical thinking. Cross-genre studies are suggested frequently to assist those instructors who prefer such studies to the genre-by-genre approach.
5. An essay suggesting a variety of ways in which students might approach textbook reading.
6. The test banks from the textbook chapters' Instructor's Manuals.
7. Sample outlines of selected textbook chapters.
8. Material that can be photocopied and used in conjunction with readings in the anthology.

The method recommended in the Instructor's Manual is practical. It not only results in measurable improvement, but it also encourages positive treatment of students. The philosophy of the approach presented in this textbook corresponds to the motto of the Scripps Howard newspapers: "Give light and the people will find their own way." The light students need is the practice of critical thinking—a tool they will need regardless of the direction they take.

Acknowledgments

Annie Todd has been remarkable. Without her tenacious involvement and stalwart support, this project would not have been completed. Janine Tangney, Melanie Opacki, and Margaret Manos have also been remarkable. I thank all of them for their enthusiasm and direction as well as their patience and flexibility.

I would also like to express my sincere appreciation to the many teachers who have contacted me to ask questions, offer suggestions, and discuss their experiences using this book. This communication has been affirming, exciting, and thought-provoking.

For more types of assistance and kindness than I could possibly name, I thank the following: Bert Andrews, Tom Ashe, Craig Beard, Tia Black, Susan Blair, Henny Bordwin, Malka Bordwin, Milton Bordwin, LaQuita Boswell, Judy Boyer, Joy Brantley, Flowers Braswell, Tom Brown, Sid Burgess, Jason Burnett, Monica Cantwell, John Coley, Stella Cocoris, Kendall Cooper, Tynes Cowan, Robby Cox, Keith Cullen, Randa Graves, Tim Douglas, Betty Duff, Barbara Enlow, Matt Fifolt, Grace Finkel, Paula Fulton, Delores Gallo, Al Gardener, Virginia Gauld, Travis Gordon, Lee Griner, John Haggerty, Lois Harris, Richard Harrison, Barbara Hill, Cindy Holmes, Helen Jackson, Jane Johnson, Jill Johnson, Diana Kato, Tracey Kell, Marilyn Kurata, Susan Labischin, Karin LaGroue, Cindy LeFoy, Pat Lisella, Marcy Ludorf, Anna Lynch, Tracy Lyons, Lisa Madison, Gaines Marsh, Haden Marsh, Randy Marsh, Stephen Marsi, Dot McCraney, Britt McCraney, Nathan McCraney, Niki McCraney, Randy McCraney, Amy McGaughey, Sue McKinnon, Susan Mitchell, Stephen Morris, Mark Myers, Rose Norman, Colm O'Dunlaing, Iris O'Dunlaing, Mary Osthoff, Jane Patton, Bob Penny, Terry Proctor, Harvey Ragland, Candace Ridington, Beebe Roberts, Dave Roberts, John Schnorrenberg, Connie Stavros, Boyce Steele, Melissa Tate, Judy Traylor, Reuben Triplett, Carol Wada, John Walker, Caroline West, Patty Wheeler-Andrews, Gayle Whidby, Barbara Williams, Debbie Williams, Natasha Womack, and Jason Womack.

Thanks as well to following reviewers: Christina Blount, *Lewis and Clark Community College*; Linda A. Caine, *Prairie State College*; Kathleen A. Carlson, *Brevard Community College*; Nandan Choksi, *American InterContinental University*; Marie Eckstrom, *Rio Hondo College*; Maria Elena Estrada, *Mt. San Antonio College*; Ann Iseda, *Jackson Community College*; Gayle Jentz, *North Hennepin Community College*; Janice Johnson, *Missouri State University*; Teresa Kozek, *Housatonic Community College*; Noreen Lace, *California State University, Northridge*; Bianca A. Lee, *Mt. San Antonio College*; Marcy Lee, *Mt. Hood Community College*; Acquelnetta Yvette Myrick, *The Community College of Baltimore County*; Karen D. O'Donnell, *Finger Lakes Community College*; Elizabeth A. O'Scanlon, *Santa Barbara City College*; Stephen W. B. Rizzo, *Bevill State Community College*; Lisa Rochford, *Sierra College*; Thomas Sadowski, *Allan Hancock College*; David A. Salomon, *The Sage Colleges*; Suzette Schlapkohl, *Scottsdale Community College*; Jacqui Shehorn, *West Hills College Lemoore*; Dayle K. Turner, *Leeward Community College*; Julie Voss, *Front Range Community College*; Shari Waldrop, *Navarro College*; Helen E. Woodman, *Ferris State University*.

Finally, I thank my students, who challenge me, inspire me, and always remind me that true learning involves reaching beyond one's grasp.

Leah McCraney

A Martian Sends a Postcard Home

Craig Raine

Caxtons are mechanical birds with many wings
and some are treasured for their markings—

they cause the eyes to melt
or the body to shriek without pain.

5   I have never seen one fly, but
sometimes they perch on the hand.

Mist is when the sky is tired of flight
and rests its soft machine on ground:

then the world is dim and bookish
10   like engravings under tissue paper.

Rain is when the earth is television.
It has the property of making colours darker.

Model T is a room with the lock inside—
a key is turned to free the world

15   for movement, so quick there is a film
to watch for anything missed.

But time is tied to the wrist
or kept in a box, ticking with impatience.

In homes, a haunted apparatus sleeps,
20   that snores when you pick it up.

If the ghost cries, they carry it
to their lips and soothe it to sleep

with sounds. And yet they wake it up
deliberately, by tickling with a finger.

25   Only the young are allowed to suffer
openly. Adults go to a punishment room

with water but nothing to eat.
They lock the door and suffer the noises

alone. No one is exempt
30   and everyone's pain has a different smell.

At night when all the colours die,
they hide in pairs

and read about themselves—
in colour, with their eyelids shut.

NOTES

Caxtons (l. 1): Literally, a caxton is any book published by William Caxton (1422–1491), the English
printer who published the first book in English (*The Recuyell of the Historyes of Troye*, 1475).

Model T (l. 13): an automobile built by Ford Motor Company from 1908 to 1927
apparatus (l. 19): device, instrument

Bedtime Story

George Macbeth

Long long ago when the world was a wild place
Planted with bushes and peopled by apes, our
Mission Brigade was at work in the jungle.
Hard by the Congo

5   Once, when a foraging detail was active
Scouting for green-fly, it came on a grey man, the
Last living man, in the branch of a baobab
Stalking a monkey

Earlier men had disposed of, for pleasure,
10   Creatures whose names we scarcely remember—
Zebra, rhinoceros, elephants, wart-hog,
Lion, rats, deer. But

After the wars had extinguished the cities
Only the wild ones were left, half-naked
15   Near the Equator: and here was the last one,
Starved for a monkey.

By then the Mission Brigade had encountered
Hundreds of such men: and their procedure.
History tells us, was only to feed them:
20   Find them and feed them;

Those were the orders. And this was the last one.
Nobody knew that he was, but he was. Mud
Caked on his flat grey flanks. He was crouched, half—
Armed with a shaved spear

25   Glinting between broad leaves. When their jaws cut
Swathes through the bark and he saw fine teeth shine,
Round eyes roll round and forked arms waver
Huge as the rough trunks

Over his head, he was frightened. Our workers
30   Marched through the Congo before he was born, but
This was the first time perhaps that he's seen one.
Starting in hot still

Silence, he crouched there: then jumped. With a long swing
Down from his branch, he had angled his spear too
35   Quickly, before they could hold him, and hurled it
Hard at the soldier

Leading the detail. How could he know the Queen's
Orders were only to help him? The soldier
Winced when the tipped spear pricked him. Unsheathing his
40   Sting was a reflex.

Later the Queen was informed. There were no more
Men. An impetuous soldier had killed off,
Purely by chance, the penultimate primate.
When she was certain

45   Squadrons of workers were fanned through the Congo
Detailed to bring back the man's picked bones to be
Sealed in the archives in amber. I'm quite sure
Nobody found them

After the most industrious search, though.
50   Where had the bones gone? Over the earth, dear,
Ground by the teeth of the termites, blown by the
Wind, like the dodo's.

NOTES

foraging (l. 5): searching (for food)
detail (l. 5): a group of soldiers assigned a specific task
swathes (l. 27): paths
unsheathing (l. 40): pulling out
impetuous (l. 43): rash; impulsive
penultimate (l. 44): next to the last
dodo (l. 53): The dodo bird was larger than a turkey and incapable of flying. It has been extinct since the late seventeenth century.

Barbie Doll

Marge Piercy

This girlchild was born as usual
and presented dolls that did pee-pee
and miniature GE stoves and irons
and wee lipsticks the color of cherry candy.
5   Then in the magic of puberty, a classmate said:
You have a great big nose and fat legs.

She was healthy, tested intelligent,
possessed strong arms and back,
abundant sexual drive and manual dexterity.
10   She went to and fro apologizing.
Everyone saw a fat nose on thick legs.

She was advised to play coy,
exhorted to come on hearty,
exercise, diet, smile and wheedle.
15   Her good nature wore out

like a fan belt.
So she cut off her nose and legs
and offered them up.

In the casket displayed on satin she lay
20   with the undertaker's cosmetics painted on,
a turned-up putty nose,
dressed in a pink and white nightie.
Doesn't she look pretty? everyone said.
Consummation at last.
25   To every woman a happy ending.

NOTES

dexterity (l. 9): skillfulness
coy (l. 12): pretended shyness or "cuteness"
exhorted (l. 13): strongly urged or advised
wheedle (l. 14): to influence by flattery
consummation (l. 24): completion or fulfillment of a goal

Mr. Z

M. Carl Holman

Taught early that his mother's skin was the sign of error,
He dressed and spoke the perfect part of honor;
Won scholarships, attended the best schools,
Disclaimed kinship with jazz and spirituals;
5   Chose prudent, raceless views for each situation,
Or when he could not cleanly skirt dissension,
Faced up to the dilemma, firmly seized
Whatever ground was Anglo-Saxonized.
In diet, too, his practice was exemplary:
10   Of pork in its profane forms he was wary;
Expert in vintage wines, sauces, and salads,
His palate shrank from cornbread, yams, and collards.

He was as careful whom he chose to kiss:
His bride had somewhere lost her Jewishness,
15   But kept her blue eyes; an Episcopalian
Prelate proclaimed them matched chameleon.
Choosing the right addresses, here, abroad,
They shunned those places where they might be barred;
Even less anxious to be asked to dine
20   Where hosts catered to kosher accent or exotic skin.
And so he climbed, unclogged by ethnic weights,
An airborne plant, flourishing without roots.
Not one false note was struck—until he died:
His subtly grieving widow could have flayed
25   The obit writers, ringing crude changes on a clumsy phrase:
"One of the most distinguished members of his race."

NOTES

disclaimed (l. 4): refused to claim

prudent (l. 5): wise, reasonable

skirt dissension (l. 6): avoid disagreement

dilemma (l. 7): a complex problem

Anglo-Saxonized (l. 8): dominated by Anglo-Saxon thinking, that is, "white" thinking

exemplary (l. 9): worth imitating

profane (l. 10): crude, coarse

wary (l. 10): cautious

vintage (l. 11): fine

palate (l. 12): taste buds

shrank from (l. 12): rejected

Prelate (l. 16): a high-ranking church official, such as a bishop

chameleon (l. 16): literally, a lizard with the ability to change its color

shunned (l. 18): avoided

barred (l. 18): not allowed to enter

catered to (l. 20): provided what was needed or desired

kosher (l. 20): literally, approved by Jewish law

exotic (l. 20): strange, different

unclogged (l. 21): freed from a difficulty

ethnic (l. 21): relating to a group of people that have certain characteristics in common, such as race, language, religion, and so on

subtly (l. 24): quietly, discreetly

flayed (l. 24): literally, to strip off the skin (as by lashing with a whip)

obit (l. 25): short for obituary, a notice of a person's death, usually with a short account of the person's life

ringing . . . changes (l. 25): running through the possible variations

distinguished (l. 26): outstanding

The Unknown Citizen

W. H. Auden

(TO JS/07/M/378 This Marble Monument Is Erected by the State)

He was found by the Bureau of Statistics to be
One against whom there was no official complaint,
And all the reports on his conduct agree
That, in the modern sense of an old-fashioned word, he was a saint,
5   For in everything he did he served the Greater Community.
Except for the War till the day he retired
He worked in a factory and never got fired,
But satisfied his employers, Fudge Motors Inc.
Yet he wasn't a scab or odd in his views,
10   For his union reports that he paid his dues,
(Our report on his Union shows it was sound)
And our Social Psychology workers found
That he was popular with his mates and liked a drink.
The Press are convinced that he bought a paper every day
15   And that his reactions to advertisements were normal in every way.
Policies taken out in his name prove that he was fully insured,
And his Health-card shows he was once in hospital but left it cured.

Both Producers Research and High-Grade Living declare
He was fully sensible to the advantages of the Installment Plan
20   And had everything necessary to the Modern Man,
A phonograph, a radio, a car and a frigidaire.
Our researchers into Public Opinion are content
That he held the proper opinions for the time of year;
When there was peace, he was for peace; when there was war, he went.
25   He was married and added five children to the population,
Which our Eugenist says was the right number for a parent of his generation.
And our teachers report that he never interfered with their education.
Was he free? Was he happy? The question is absurd:
Had anything been wrong, we should certainly have heard.

NOTES

scab (l. 9): a worker who will not join a labor union or who takes a striker's job
Installment Plan (l. 19): a plan in which goods are paid for over a period of time
frigidaire (l. 21): a refrigerator
Eugenist: (l. 26): an expert on the production of healthy offspring
absurd (l. 28): ridiculous

Curiosity

Alastair Reid

may have killed the cat; more likely
the cat was just unlucky, or else curious
to see what death was like, having no cause
to go on licking paws, or fathering

5   litter on litter of kittens, predictably.
Nevertheless, to be curious
is dangerous enough. To distrust
what is always said, what seems,
to ask odd questions, interfere in dreams,

10   leave home, smell rats, have hunches
do not endear cats to those doggy circles
where well-smelt baskets, suitable wives, good lunches
are the order of things, and where prevails
much wagging of incurious heads and tails.

15   Face it. Curiosity
will not cause us to die—
only lack of it will.
Never to want to see
the other side of the hill
20   or that improbable country
where living is an idyll
(although a probable hell)
would kill us all.
Only the curious

25 have, if they live, a tale
    worth telling at all.

    Dogs say cats love too much, are irresponsible,
    are changeable, marry too many wives,
    desert their children, chill all dinner tables
30 with tales of their nine lives.
    Well, they are lucky. Let them be
    nine-lived and contradictory,
    curious enough to change, prepared to pay
    the cat price, which is to die
35 and die again and again,
    each time with no less pain.
    A cat minority of one
    is all that can be counted on
    to tell the truth. And what cats have to tell
40 on each return from hell
    is this: that dying is what the living do,
    that dying is what the loving do,
    and that dead dogs are those who do not know
    that dying is what, to live, each has to do.

NOTE

idyll (l. 21): a simple, peaceful, or carefree existence

The History Teacher

Billy Collins

    Trying to protect his students' innocence
    he told them the Ice Age was really just
    the Chilly Age, a period of a million years
    when everyone had to wear sweaters.

5   And the Stone Age became the Gravel Age,
    named after the long driveways of the time.

    The Spanish Inquisition was nothing more
    than an outbreak of questions such as
    "How far is it from here to Madrid?"
10 "What do you call the matador's hat?"

    The War of the Roses took place in a garden,
    and the Enola Gay dropped one tiny atom on Japan.

    The children would leave his classroom
    for the playground to torment the weak
15 and the smart,
    mussing up their hair and breaking their glasses,

    while he gathered up his notes and walked home
    past flower beds and white picket fences,

20   wondering if they would believe that soldiers
      in the Boer War told long, rambling stories
      designed to make the enemy nod off.

NOTES

Ice Age (l. 2): During the Ice Age (approximately 2 million BCE to 10,000 BCE), much of the world was covered by sheets of ice. Humans first appeared during this epoch.

Stone Age (l.5): During the Stone Age (approximately 700,000 BCE to 8,000 BCE), humans began creating tools out of stone.

Spanish Inquisition (l.7): The Spanish Inquisition began as an effort to protect Catholicism in Spain from the growing population of Muslims and Jews during the fifteenth century. Spanish citizens were questioned and often tortured in an effort to identify and convert Jews, Muslims, or Catholics lacking in faith.

outbreak (l. 8): epidemic

Madrid (l. 9): the capital of Spain, and its largest city

Matador's (l. 10): lead bullfighter's

War of the Roses (l. 11): a series of battles waged from 1455 to 1485 between the families of York and Lancaster for the right to claim England's throne

Enola Gay (l. 12): the B-29 bomber that flew over Hiroshima, Japan, on Aug. 6, 1945, and dropped the first atomic bomb, nicknamed "Little Boy," to force Japan to surrender to the Allies to end World War II

torment (l. 14): harass and hurt

mussing (l. 16): messing up

Boer War (l.20): The Boer War collectively identifies two separate conflicts between the Dutch Boers and the British colonists in South Africa. The first Boer War (1880–1881) was waged by the Boers to regain the land and political freedoms they traded to Britain in exchange for Britain's help in their fight against the Zulu. The second Boer War (1899–1902) was fought when two neighboring Boer states declared war on Britain over commercial access to the gold and diamond mines in the area.

rambling (l. 20): pointless

nod off (l. 21): fall asleep

The Chimney Sweeper, from *Songs of Innocence*
William Blake

When my mother died I was very young,
And my father sold me while yet my tongue
Could scarcely cry "'weep! 'weep! 'weep! 'weep!"
So your chimneys I sweep & in soot I sleep.

5   There's little Tom Dacre, who cried when his head,
      That curl'd like a lamb's back, was shav'd, so I said,
      "Hush, Tom! never mind it, for when your head's bare,
      You know that the soot cannot spoil your white hair."

      And so he was quiet, & that very night,
10   As Tom was a-sleeping he had such a sight!
      That thousands of sweepers, Dick, Joe, Ned, & Jack,
      Were all of them lock'd up in coffins of black;

      And by came an Angel who had a bright key,
      And he open'd the coffins & set them all free;
15   Then down a green plain, leaping, laughing they run,
      And wash in a river and shine in the Sun.

ride (l. 8): car
dig (l. 10): understand
License and registration (l. 32): driver's license and proof of owning the car
North Star (l. 34): Here, *North Star* refers literally to the emblem on the police officer's car door. The reference, however, has broader significance. The North Star, the brightest star in the Little Dipper constellation, has historically been used by travelers and sailors to determine which way is north. Fleeing slaves used it to find their way to the antislavery states of the North. Frederick Douglass's antislavery newspaper (published from 1847 to 1851) was called *North Star.*
déjà vu (l. 34): the feeling an event has occurred before
bruthas (l. 48): black men

Parsley

Rita Dove

I. The Cane Fields

There is a parrot imitating spring
in the palace, its feathers parsley green.
Out of the swamp the cane appears

to haunt us, and we cut it down. El General
5   searches for a word; he is all the world
there is. Like a parrot imitating spring,

we lie down screaming as rain punches through
and we come up green. We cannot speak an R—
out of the swamp, the cane appears

10   and then the mountain we call in whispers *Katalina.*
The children gnaw their teeth to arrowheads.
There is a parrot imitating spring.

El General has found his word: *perejil.*
Who says it, lives. He laughs, teeth shining
15   out of the swamp. The cane appears

in our dreams, lashed by wind and streaming.
And we lie down. For every drop of blood
there is a parrot imitating spring.
Out of the swamp the cane appears.

2. The Palace

20   The word the general's chosen is parsley.
It is fall, when thoughts turn
to love and death; the general thinks
of his mother, how she died in the fall
and he planted her walking cane at the grave

25   and it flowered, each spring stolidly forming
four-star blossoms. The general

pulls on his boots, he stomps to
her room in the palace, the one without
curtains, the one with a parrot
30   in a brass ring. As he paces he wonders
Who can I kill today. And for a moment
the little knot of screams
is still. The parrot, who has traveled

all the way from Australia in an ivory
35   cage, is, coy as a widow, practising
spring. Ever since the morning
his mother collapsed in the kitchen
while baking skull-shaped candies
for the Day of the Dead, the general
40   has hated sweets. He orders pastries
brought up for the bird; they arrive

dusted with sugar on a bed of lace.
The knot in his throat starts to twitch;
he sees his boots the first day in battle
45   splashed with mud and urine
as a soldier falls at his feet amazed—
how stupid he looked!—at the sound
of artillery. *I never thought it would sing*
the soldier said, and died. Now

50   the general sees the fields of sugar
cane, lashed by rain and streaming.
He sees his mother's smile, the teeth
gnawed to arrowheads. He hears
the Haitians sing without R's
55   as they swing the great machetes:
Katalina, they sing, *Katalina*,

mi madle, mi amol en muelte. God knows
his mother was no stupid woman; she
could roll an R like a queen. Even
60   a parrot can roll an R! In the bare room
the bright feathers arch in a parody
of greenery, as the last pale crumbs
disappear under the blackened tongue. Someone

calls out his name in a voice
65   so like his mother's, a startled tear
splashes the tip of his right boot.
My mother, my love in death.
The general remembers the tiny green sprigs

men of his village wore in their capes
70   to honor the birth of a son. He will
order many, this time, to be killed

for a single, beautiful word.

NOTES

"On October 2, 1937, Rafael Trujillo (1891–1961), dictator of the Dominican Republic, ordered 20,000 blacks killed because they could not pronounce the letter 'r' in *perejil*, the Spanish word for parsley." [Dove's note]

El General (l. 4): Trujillo was called *El Jefe* ("The Chief").

Katalina (l. 10): The Haitian pronunciation of *Katarina*. The "r" in the Haitians' native French-based Creole language is not trilled as it is in Spanish (the native language of Dominicans).

The children gnaw their teeth to arrowheads (l. 11): Gnawing on sugarcane can grind teeth into sharp points.

perejil (l. 13) the Spanish word for parsley

coy (l. 35): flirtatiously shy

Baking skull-shaped candies . . . for the Day of the Dead (l. 38–39): The Day of the Dead is a Latin American holiday designed to honor dead relatives as well as the continuity of life. It is traditional to bake dough into skull-shaped cookies called *pan de muerto* or "bread of the dead."

mi madle, mi amol en muelte (l. 57): the Haitian pronunciation of *mi madre, mi amore en muerte*, Spanish for *My mother, my love in death* (l. 67)

arch (l. 61): curve

parody (l. 61): poor imitation

What Would Freud Say?

Bob Hicok

Wasn't on purpose that I drilled
through my finger or the nurse
laughed. She apologized
three times and gave me a shot
5   of something that was a lusher
apology. The person
who drove me home
said my smile was a smeared
totem that followed
10   his body that night as it arced
over a cliff in a dream.
He's always flying
in his dreams and lands
on cruise ships or hovers
15   over Atlanta with an erection.
He put me to bed and the drugs
wore off and I woke
to cannibals at my extremities.
I woke with a sense
20   of what nails in the palms
might do to a spirit
temporarily confined to flesh.

That too was an accident
if you believe Judas
25   merely wanted to be loved.
To be loved by God,
Urban the 8th
had heads cut off
that were inadequately
30   bowed by dogma. To be loved
by Blondie, Dagwood
gets nothing right
except the hallucinogenic
architecture of sandwiches.
35   He would have drilled
through a finger too
while making a case for books
on home repair and health.
Drilling through my finger's
40   not the dumbest thing
I've done. Second place
was approaching
a frozen gas-cap with lighter
in hand while thinking
45   *heat melts ice* and not
explosion kills asshole. First
place was passing
through a bedroom door
and removing silk that did not
50   belong to my wife.
Making a bookcase is not
the extent of my apology.
I've also been beaten up
in a bar for saying huevos
55   rancheros in a way
insulting to the patrons'
ethnicity. I've also lost
my job because lying
face down on the couch
60   didn't jibe with my employer's
definition of home
office. I wanted her to come
through the door on Sunday
and see the bookcase
65   she'd asked me to build
for a year and be impressed
that it didn't lean
or wobble even though
I've only leaned and often

70   wobbled. Now it's half
      done but certainly
      a better gift with its map
      of my unfaithful blood.

NOTES

lusher (l. 5): more delicious

totem (l. 9): literally, an object, plant, or animal that serves as a symbol of a family or clan

arced (l. 10): moved in an arc (the outer circumference of a circle)

extremities (l. 18): fingers and toes

Judas (l. 24): the apostle who betrayed Jesus (Matthew 26:14–15, 26:47–50, 27:1–5; Mark 14:10–11, 14:43–45; Luke 22:1–6, 22:47–49; John 131–3, 13:21–30, 18:1–8; Acts 1:18–20)

Urban the 8th (l. 27): the Pope (1623–1644) who persecuted Galileo Galilei (1564–1642) for supporting Copernicus's theory that all planets revolved around the sun, thus challenging the Catholic Church's teaching that the sun and other planets revolved around the earth

dogma (l. 30): a church's formal religious principles

Blondie, Dagwood (l. 31): characters from a popular comic strip that focuses on a suburban family headed by the bumbling Dagwood and his beautiful wife Blondie

huevos rancheros (l. 54–55): a Mexican dish comprised of eggs, onion, tomatoes, garlic, chili peppers, and cheese, served on tortillas. The speaker likely misspoke and asked for *huevos de rancheros*—"rancher's testicles"—instead of *huevos rancheros*.

jibe (l. 60): agree with

2
Fiction

Birthday Party ✓

Katharine Brush

1   They were a couple in their late thirties, and they looked unmistakably married. They sat on the banquette opposite us in a little narrow restaurant, having dinner. The man had a round, self-satisfied face, with glasses on it; the woman was fadingly pretty, in a big hat. There was nothing conspicuous about them, nothing particularly noticeable, until the end of their meal, when it suddenly became obvious that this was an Occasion—in fact, the husband's birthday, and the wife had planned a little surprise for him.

2   It arrived, in the form of a small but glossy birthday cake, with one pink candle burning in the center. The headwaiter brought it in and placed it before the husband, and meanwhile the violin-and-piano orchestra played "Happy Birthday to You," and the wife beamed with shy pride over her little surprise, and such few people as there were in the restaurant tried to help out with a pattering of applause. It became clear at once that help was needed, because the husband was not pleased. Instead he was hotly embarrassed, and indignant at his wife for embarrassing him.

3   You looked at him and saw this and you thought, "Oh, now don't *be* like that!" But he was like that, and as soon as the little cake had been deposited on the table, and the orchestra had finished the birthday piece, and the general attention had shifted from the man and woman, I saw him say something to her under his breath—some punishing thing, quick and curt and unkind. I couldn't bear to look at the woman then, so I stared at my plate and waited for quite a long time. Not long enough, though. She was still crying when I finally glanced over there again. Crying quietly and heartbrokenly and hopelessly, all to herself, under the gay big brim of her best hat.

NOTES

banquette (par. 1): an upholstered bench along a wall

indignant (par. 2): angry

The Lottery ✓

Shirley Jackson

1   The morning of June 27th was clear and sunny, with the fresh warmth of a full-summer day; the flowers were blossoming profusely and the grass was richly green. The people of the village began to gather in the square, between the post office and the bank, around ten o'clock; in some towns there were so many people that the lottery took two days and had to be started on June 26th, but in this village, where there were only about three hundred people,

NOTE

profusely (par. 1): in great quantity

---

184   The doctor inspects Gabe.

185   "There's something strange. About his weight," Julia says.

186   "I'm not really concerned about that right now," the doctor says. "I'd rather focus on this." She gestures at Gabe's arms, then his chest, then the back of his head.

187   "What? I don't see anything."

188   "Bruising. It's common, at this age, when they're first crawling around and bumping into things, but . . . "

189   "He doesn't crawl around," Julia says. "He just sits there."

190   The doctor looks at her probingly. "Are you sure you're not being too rough with him?" she says. "You might be hurting him without realizing it."

191   "I'd know! He'd tell me!" Julia says hotly, privately wondering how. Write little notes? Use sign language?

192   The doctor is silent so long that they both hear Julia's stomach make a squealing, spiraling sound.

193   "Just remember to be gentle," the doctor says finally. "Watch the bruises." She makes Julia look closely, pointing out the blacker-than-black marks that she says are sore spots. She talks about the "thumb-shaped" bruises on his chest, and the "finger-sized" ones on his back. "I'd like to do another cat scan," she says, but just then an unearthly howling arises from another examining room. The doctor dashes out, and Julia grabs Gabe and his clothes and flees.

194   "Jonas?"

195   "What?"

196   "Nothing."

197   He looks different. He's shaved something off, or let something grow. Why is everyone changing their hair all of a sudden? The difference is that he's clean-shaven, she decides, rather than sporting his usual half-grown stubble. His eyebrows look groomed. And his eyelashes are gone. Has he never had eyelashes? How could she not notice something like that? The absence of hair ought to reveal more of him, but somehow it has the opposite effect: his face seems harder, smoother, more artificial, a rigid mask.

198   "Jonas?"

199   "What?"

200   She looks at his hands. They're thick, blunt, made for crushing things or wrenching them apart. She should leave. She should just leave, right now. Instead she runs her finger down his cheek. It's as soft as suède.

201   They make love on the couch. Jonas moves so slowly, so gently, he doesn't break a sweat. Gabe watches the whole thing from his bouncy-swing. He's so heavy he doesn't bounce, just hangs suspended, the frame buckling under his deadweight.

202   The second time Gabe vanishes she knows she shouldn't panic. But she does. She panics more than she did the first time. Again she dashes up and down stairs, wheeling and whirling, her own hysterical breathing drowning out all other sound. Finally she stops, pauses, tries to feel on her skin the tiny air currents stirred up by movement somewhere in the house.

NOTES

probingly (par. 190): searchingly

deadweight (par. 201): heavy, motionless weight

203   She finds him sitting in the empty bathtub, not crying, not lost in contemplation of his warped reflection in the faucet, as a normal baby would be. He's sitting, hands folded, patient, simply waiting.

204   She lugs him to his changing table, whips off his playsuit, his diaper, turns on a bright lamp, and inspects him all over. She thinks she sees a new bruise on his ankle, then one on his groin. Then a ring of small ones flowering on his shoulder like a bite mark. Then one on his cheek. Then she's seeing them everywhere, his whole hide is mottled with them, coated with them.

205   "I give up," she says.

206   She hears Jonas slam the front door. "Baby," he calls. "Baby, darling, mother dear, shoogums, sweetheart, honey pie, sugar lips, babycakes, cinnamon roll"—reciting the litany of eons ago, back when he was always kidding but meant it all and she didn't believe a word of it. She feels a frantic desire to hide—hide herself, hide Gabe, fold up the entire house and hide it in her pocket. She crouches over the changing table and hears Jonas's footsteps on the stairs. She is conscious of her exposed back, the vulnerability of her nape and skull.

207   She tells herself that there is a masked intruder coming down the hall. That fantasy is preferable to the truth.

208   "Honey," he says. "I'm home."

209   She wakes feeling that something is wrong. She wakes to vertigo every morning, but today is different.

210   She trudges to the nursery, rotating her sore shoulders, cracking her back. The rocking chair nods gently, as if someone had just vacated it. The astronauts and cowboys and lion tamers on the wallpaper wink at her. Jonas picked the paper; she had been skeptical. The astronauts have what are unquestionably codpieces attached to their spacesuits, and the lion tamers seem a little too fey. For the hundredth time she resolves to repaper the room. She leans over the crib.

211   A pink-skinned, black-haired green-eyed baby looks back at her. She screams. The baby screams. It's so loud, she's never heard anything so loud, it's like the walls are screaming.

212   Jonas comes running. He comes just a little too quickly, as if he'd been waiting a few steps down the hall; his surprise is a bit too theatrical.

213   "Where is Gabe?" she screams. "Where is he?"

NOTES

contemplation (par. 203): thoughtful observation

mottled (par. 204): marked

litany (par. 206): long list

eons (par. 206): long time

nape (par. 206): back (of the neck)

vertigo (par. 209): dizziness

trudges (par. 210): walks heavily

skeptical (par. 210): doubtful

codpieces (par. 210): a pouch at the crotch of the tight fitting pants men wore in the fifteenth and sixteenth centuries

fey (par. 210): fairylike

214   Jonas's face shifts from blankness to surprise to ecstatic realization in a metamorphosis that has clearly been rehearsed for hours before the bathroom mirror. "But this is Gabe. He's changed. He's cured."

215   "This is not Gabe! Have you lost your mind? Where did this baby come from?"

216   "It's a miracle. He finally changed. I knew he would. He's healed."

217   "He wasn't sick! He was fine before!"

218   "He's normal now. We can be a normal family. Isn't that what you wanted?"

219   "What you wanted."

220   The baby's eyes flick back and forth; fists wave in the air; legs kick. A new sound comes out of its mouth. Not a scream. Something else. The audible language of babies is so foreign to her she doesn't understand what's happening. Jonas lifts the baby and holds it against his shoulder, and the noise stops.

221   "What is going on?"

222   A loud burp mocks her. Jonas? Or the baby?

223   "Why can't you just be happy?" Jonas says.

224   And that's what everyone tells her: the doctors, the police when she insists on calling them, her parents, their friends. It's a miracle, people say. You should consider yourselves lucky. Just one of those things. Even the doctors say this.

225   "Don't put a gift horse in your mouth, right?" Jonas says. "Count your blessings, right? Didn't you say that?" The new baby vomits great lumpy gouts on her shoulder. He has mushy features, a fat chin—nothing like Gabe's. He's light, flabby, insubstantial. She could toss him out the window if she wanted to. She might. He screams and screams. His face turns red when he screams, when he burps, when the slightest flicker of emotion or indigestion ripples through him.

226   "Like you," Jonas says. Which is true; when Julia gets embarrassed or excited, red splotches appear on her throat and chest, as if she were being throttled by an invisible strangler. She's splotchy now.

227   "Why can't you accept a good thing?" Jonas asks. "I can understand being in denial about a tragedy, but not this. Why do you have to question it?"

228   "This is not my baby," she says. No one listens.

229   But she knows. A mother knows. Her breasts ache. Her longing for Gabe is intensely physical, a barbed fishhook tugging.

230   The strange baby sucks at her, eating her up. That's not yours, she wants to tell him. It's on loan, it belongs to someone else. When he comes back, you'll have to repay the debt somehow.

NOTES

ecstatic (par. 214): joyful

metamorphosis (par. 214): rapid and complete change

Don't put a gift horse in your mouth (par. 225): The phrase is actually "Don't look a gift horse in the mouth," meaning, "Don't question or reject opportunity and good fortune."

gouts (par. 225): large blobs

insubstantial (par. 225): lacking substance

throttled (par. 226): choked

denial (par. 227): In psychology, *denial* refers to the unconscious refusal to admit painful truths, thoughts, or feelings.

231   She tells herself she is a wet nurse, as in medieval times, suckling the queen's child. It's a job, that's all.

232   "It was just a phase," Jonas says. "He outgrew it." He's full of authority all of a sudden. Doesn't he ever go to work anymore? Seems like he's always here, changing diapers, wiping everything down with antiseptic cleaners, plying the baby with soft goggle-eyed toys.

233   She surreptitiously rifles the house, every baby-sized space she can think of. She peers into the clothes dryer with a flashlight before using it.

234   With the baby on her shoulder, she searches the back yard for spots of freshly turned-up earth. She's being morbid, she knows.

235   She finds a soft patch and begins digging at it with the toe of her sneaker. The dirt comes away easily. It would be quicker with a shovel, but she doesn't want to put the baby down and go get one. She can't leave the baby in the house, she needs him here, she needs him to see, bear witness. She must maintain balance, at all costs. Whatever hole she finds Gabe in, she will take him out and leave this strange baby in his place.

236   She's still kicking and scooping with her foot when Jonas comes home. Headlights. Door slamming. Lights go on in rooms, she hears his voice faintly calling. She sees the light go on in the nursery, now she sees his flitting, panicked shadow. She should call to him. But not yet, not yet, she'll watch the show a minute longer. That must be what I looked like, she thinks, when I found Gabe missing.

237   Something catches his eye, her white shirt, probably, moving against the darkening hedges. He comes racing outside, little loose bits of him—hair, shirt collar, glasses, jowls—jiggling and fluttering.

238   He looks at her, the baby, the breadbox-size hole. "What are you doing?"

239   "I thought . . . I thought . . . "

240   "I know what you thought. Can't you see how silly you're being?"

241   Yes, she thinks, I underestimated you. Of course you wouldn't hide him here, right under our noses.

242   "What do we have to do," he says, "to make you happy?"

243   "You know."

244   "Listen," he sighs. "What if I stop trying to convince you that this is Gabe? Why don't we pretend that this is another kid, who's just dropped in our laps and we have to take care of him. Would that make it easier?"

245   "No," she says, staring at his teeth, which are blue in the twilight. She rubs the baby's back. He burrows his way into her neck and glues himself there with drool. Jonas is right; it'll be far easier to be charitable and love a strange child than to surrender her convictions and concede that he's really hers.

NOTES

wet nurse (par. 231): a woman who breast feeds another woman's child

suckling (par. 231): breast feeding

plying (par. 232): providing

surreptitiously (par. 233): secretly

rifles (par. 233): searches through

being morbid (par. 234): preoccupied with unwholesome and gloomy thoughts

jowls (par. 237): cheeks

concede (par. 245): admit

246   But she finds that the former begins to gradually lead her to the latter, in a slow and insidious way. As days and weeks pass, she relaxes into routines, takes pleasure in the baby's burps and crows and crawling, and forgets for long traitorous periods about her real son. And then it's not a forgetting; she begins to suspect that everyone is right and she is wrong, that this is Gabe after all.

247   Am I going to react this violently every time he changes? she asks herself. Am I going to be one of those mothers who can't bear their children to grow up, even a little bit?

248   She begins to think she sees him, her Gabe, in this baby. Truly in him; she glimpses the shimmer of Gabe's pale eyes behind the baby's greenish ones, the glint of gold beneath the scalp, like hairs trapped beneath stockings.

249   Impossible, she thinks. But she can't shake the idea.

250   How clever of Jonas, she thinks, to hide him in plain sight.

251   Impossible.

252   But they smell the same, don't they? This baby and Gabe. She searches her library of sense memories. And the teeth, the teeth are exactly the same. Jonas never even knew about the teeth. He couldn't have known to find a replacement baby with the exact same—

253   Gabe's in there, she thinks, he's been inside there all along. Trapped. Trying to signal to her, calling silently. She puts an ear to the baby's chest.

254   She tries to put the thoughts aside but they bounce back up like balloons. What does it matter, she thinks. If Gabe is in there, then she should be glad to have him, in any form. But she wants proof. She wants to be sure.

255   A strange line of thought arises, which she tries to erase, but can't. She has sudden urges, imagines smashing the baby like a vase to see what's inside, imagines unscrewing his head like the top of a perfume bottle. Changing his diaper, she pulls his legs apart to clean him and imagines pulling, and pulling, and pulling.

256   She has to lay her suspicions to rest, once and for all. If she could just lift up a bit of skin and see—

257   This pale skin that has grown up over him like a crust, a chrysalis—

258   Just peel back a corner, like getting a peek at the old wallpaper—

259   Just a peek–then she will be at peace. Then she will lay down her arms, she will concede everything. She will be the best mother the world has ever seen.

260   Just a little bit. She'll be so gentle, he won't even feel it. Quick, now, before she loses her nerve. Gabe darling, if that's you in there, just lie still, Mommy's coming—

NOTES

insidious (par. 246): tempting, but dangerous

traitorous (par. 246): disloyal

glint (par. 248): flash

chrysalis (par. 257): The developmental stage between caterpillar and butterfly or moth that is most recognized by the cocoon in which it is encased. Sometimes, as here, the term *chrysalis* refers to the actual cocoon.

lay down her arms (par. 259): surrender

261   Jonas has left work early—no reason, just felt something was wrong at home, first stirrings of the parent's sixth sense. He checks the yard, then clatters through the house, vaults up the stairs. Now he pauses in the doorway of the nursery and sees a woman he doesn't recognize, a woman with only the vaguest resemblance to his wife, hunched over the baby on the changing table. The baby is silent, as if curious, waiting. The changeling mother bends studiously to her work, moments away from discovery, revelation, reunion. The baby holds his breath.

NOTES

vaguest (par. 261): slightest
changeling (par. 261): literally, a child secretly left in place of another child

The Veldt

Ray Bradbury

1   "George, I wish you'd look at the nursery."

2   "What's wrong with it?"

3   "I don't know."

4   "Well, then."

5   "I just want you to look at it, is all, or call a psychologist in to look at it."

6   "What would a psychologist want with a nursery?"

7   "You know very well what he'd want." His wife paused in the middle of the kitchen and watched the stove busy humming to itself, making supper for four.

8   "It's just that the nursery is different now than it was."

9   "All right, let's have a look."

10   They walked down the hall of their soundproofed, Happylife Home, which had cost them thirty thousand dollars installed, this house which clothed and fed and rocked them to sleep and played and sang and was good to them. Their approach sensitized a switch somewhere and the nursery light flicked on when they came within ten feet of it. Similarly, behind them, in the halls, lights went on and off as they left them behind, with a soft automaticity.

11   "Well," said George Hadley.

12   They stood on the thatched floor of the nursery. It was forty feet across by forty feet long and thirty feet high; it had cost half again as much as the rest of the house. "But nothing's too good for our children," George had said.

13   The nursery was silent. It was empty as a jungle glade at hot high noon. The walls were blank and two dimensional. Now, as George and Lydia Hadley

NOTES

Veldt (title): grassland
thatched (par. 12): straw covered
glade (par. 13): an open space in the middle of a forest
two dimensional (par. 13): having height and width

stood in the center of the room, the walls began to purr and recede into crystalline distance, it seemed, and presently an African veldt appeared, in three dimensions; on all sides, in colors reproduced to the final pebble and bit of straw. The ceiling above them became a deep sky with a hot yellow sun.

14   George Hadley felt the perspiration start on his brow.

15   "Let's get out of the sun," he said. "This is a little too real. But I don't see anything wrong."

16   "Wait a moment, you'll see," said his wife.

17   Now the hidden odorophonics were beginning to blow a wind of odor at the two people in the middle of the baked veldtland. The hot straw smell of lion grass, the cool green smell of the hidden water hole, the great rusty smell of animals, the smell of dust like a red paprika in the hot air. And now the sounds: the thump of distant antelope feet on grassy sod, the papery rustling of vultures. A shadow passed through the sky. The shadow flickered on George Hadley's upturned, sweating face.

18   "Filthy creatures," he heard his wife say.

19   "The vultures."

20   "You see, there are the lions, far over, that way. Now they're on their way to the water hole. They've just been eating," said Lydia. "I don't know what."

21   "Some animal." George Hadley put his hand up to shield off the burning light from his squinted eyes. "A zebra or a baby giraffe, maybe."

22   "Are you sure?" His wife sounded peculiarly tense.

23   "No, it's a little late to be sure," he said, amused. "Nothing over there I can see but cleaned bone, and the vultures dropping for what's left."

24   "Did you hear that scream?" she asked.

25   "No."

26   "About a minute ago?"

27   "Sorry, no."

28   The lions were coming. And again George Hadley was filled with admiration for the mechanical genius who had conceived this room. A miracle of efficiency selling for an absurdly low price. Every home should have one. Oh, occasionally they frightened you with their clinical accuracy, they startled you, gave you a twinge, but most of the time what fun for everyone, not only your own son and daughter, but for yourself when you felt like a quick jaunt to a foreign land, a quick change of scenery. Well, here it was!

29   And here were the lions now, fifteen feet away, so real, so feverishly and startlingly real that you could feel the prickling fur on your hand, and your mouth was stuffed with the dusty upholstery smell of their heated pelts, and the yellow of them was in your eyes like the yellow of an exquisite French tapestry, the yellows of lions and summer grass, and the sound of the matted lion lungs exhaling on the silent noontide, and the smell of meat from the panting, dripping mouths.

NOTES

recede into crystalline distance (par. 13): become transparent

three dimensions (par. 13): having height, width, and depth

jaunt (par. 28): pleasure trip

tapestry (par. 29): a heavy cloth woven with designs, frequently used as a wall hanging

30   The lions stood looking at George and Lydia Hadley with terrible green-yellow eyes.

31   "Watch out!" screamed Lydia.

32   The lions came running at them.

33   Lydia bolted and ran. Instinctively, George sprang after her. Outside, in the hall, with the door slammed, he was laughing and she was crying, and they both stood appalled at the other's reaction.

34   "George!"

35   "Lydia! Oh, my dear poor sweet Lydia!"

36   "They almost got us!"

37   "Walls, Lydia, remember; crystal walls, that's all they are. Oh, they look real, I must admit—Africa in your parlor—but it's all dimensional superreactionary, supersensitive color film and mental tape film behind glass screens. It's all odorophonics and sonics, Lydia. Here's my handkerchief."

38   "I'm afraid." She came to him and put her body against him and cried steadily. "Did you see? Did you *feel*? It's too real."

39   "Now, Lydia . . . "

40   "You've got to tell Wendy and Peter not to read any more on Africa."

41   "Of course—of course." He patted her.

42   "Promise?"

43   "Sure."

44   "And lock the nursery for a few days until I get my nerves settled."

45   "You know how difficult Peter is about that. When I punished him a month ago by locking the nursery for even a few hours—the tantrum he threw! And Wendy too. They *live* for the nursery."

46   "It's got to be locked, that's all there is to it."

47   "All right." Reluctantly he locked the huge door. "You've been working too hard. You need a rest."

48   "I don't know—I don't know," she said, blowing her nose, sitting down in a chair that immediately began to rock and comfort her. "Maybe I don't have enough to do. Maybe I have time to think too much. Why don't we shut the whole house off for a few days and take a vacation?"

49   "You mean you want to fry my eggs for me?"

50   "Yes." She nodded.

51   "And darn my socks?"

52   "Yes." A frantic, watery-eyed nodding.

53   "And sweep the house?"

54   "Yes, yes—oh, yes!"

55   "But I thought that's why we bought this house, so we wouldn't have to do anything?"

56   "That's just it. I feel like I don't belong here. The house is wife and mother now and nursemaid. Can I compete with an African veldt? Can I give a bath

NOTES

bolted (par. 33): jerked, moved suddenly
appalled (par. 33): shocked

and scrub the children as efficiently or quickly as the automatic scrub bath can? I cannot. And it isn't just me. It's you. You've been awfully nervous lately."

57   "I suppose I have been smoking too much."

58   "You look as if you didn't know what to do with yourself in this house, either. You smoke a little more every morning and drink a little more every afternoon and need a little more sedative every night. You're beginning to feel unnecessary too."

59   "Am I?" He paused and tried to feel into himself to see what was really there.

60   "Oh, George!" She looked beyond him, at the nursery door: "Those lions can't get out of there, can they?"

61   He looked at the door and saw it tremble as if something had jumped against it from the other side.

62   "Of course not," he said.

63   At dinner they ate alone, for Wendy and Peter were at a special plastic carnival across town and had televised home to say they'd be late, to go ahead eating. So George Hadley, bemused, sat watching the dining-room table produce warm dishes of food from its mechanical interior.

64   "We forgot the ketchup," he said.

65   "Sorry," said a small voice within the table, and ketchup appeared.

66   As for the nursery, thought George Hadley, it won't hurt for the children to be locked out of it awhile. Too much of anything isn't good for anyone. And it was clearly indicated that the children had been spending a little too much time on Africa. That sun. He could feel it on his neck, still, like a hot paw. And the lions. And the smell of blood. Remarkable how the nursery caught the telepathic emanations of the children's minds and created life to fill their every desire. The children thought lions, and there were lions. The children thought zebras, and there were zebras. Sun—sun. Giraffes—giraffes. Death and death.

67   That last. He chewed tastelessly on the meat that the table had cut for him. Death thoughts. They were awfully young, Wendy and Peter, for death thoughts. Or, no, you were never too young, really. Long before you knew what death was you were wishing it on someone else. When you were two years old you were shooting people with cap pistols.

68   But this—the long, hot African veldt—the awful death in the jaws of a lion. And repeated again and again.

69   "Where are you going?"

70   He didn't answer Lydia. Preoccupied, he let the lights glow softly on ahead of him, extinguished behind him as he padded to the nursery door. He listened against it. Far away, a lion roared.

71   He unlocked the door and opened it. Just before he stepped inside, he heard a faraway scream. And then another roar from the lions, which subsided quickly.

NOTES

bemused (par. 63): lost in thought

telepathic emanations (par. 66): thoughts

subsided (par. 71): stopped

72   He stepped into Africa. How many times in the last year had he opened this door and found Wonderland, Alice, the Mock Turtle, or Aladdin and his Magical Lamp, or Jack Pumpkinhead of Oz, or Dr. Doolittle, or the cow jumping over a very real-appearing moon—all the delightful contraptions of a make-believe world. How often had he seen Pegasus flying in the sky ceiling, or seen fountains of red fireworks, or heard angel voices singing. But now, this yellow hot Africa, this bake oven with murder in the heat. Perhaps Lydia was right. Perhaps they needed a little vacation from the fantasy which was growing a bit too real for ten-year-old children. It was all right to exercise one's mind with gymnastic fantasies, but when the lively child mind settled on *one* pattern . . . ? It seemed that, at a distance, for the past month, he had heard lions roaring, and smelled their strong odor seeping as far away as his study door. But, being busy, he had paid it no attention.

73   George Hadley stood on the African grassland alone. The lions looked up from their feeding, watching him. The only flaw to the illusion was the open door through which he could see his wife, far down the dark hall, like a framed picture, eating her dinner abstractedly.

74   "Go away," he said to the lions.

75   They did not go.

76   He knew the principle of the room exactly. You sent out your thoughts. Whatever you thought would appear.

77   "Let's have Aladdin and his lamp," he snapped.

78   The veldtland remained; the lions remained.

79   "Come on, room! I demand Aladdin!" he said.

80   Nothing happened. The lions mumbled in their baked pelts.

81   "Aladdin!"

82   He went back to dinner. "The fool room's out of order," he said. "It won't respond."

83   "Or—"

84   "Or what?"

85   "Or it *can't* respond," said Lydia, "because the children have thought about Africa and lions and killing so many days that the room's in a rut."

86   "Could be."

87   "Or Peter's set it to remain that way."

88   "*Set* it?"

89   "He may have got into the machinery and fixed something."

90   "Peter doesn't know machinery."

91   "He's a wise one for ten. That I.Q. of his—"

92   "Nevertheless—"

93   "Hello, Mom. Hello, Dad."

NOTES

Wonderland, Alice . . . moon (par. 72): places and characters from children's stories

contraptions (par. 72): inventions

Pegasus (par. 72): a winged horse in Greek mythology

85   She sprang out of bed. "Yeah, Joe. Ah didn't reckon you wuz hongry."

86   No need to die today. Joe needed her for a few more minutes anyhow.

87   Soon there was a roaring fire in the cook stove. Water bucket full and two chickens killed. Joe loved fried chicken and rice. She didn't deserve a thing and good Joe was letting her cook him some breakfast. She rushed hot biscuits to the table as Joe took his seat.

88   He ate with his eyes on his plate. No laughter, no banter.

89   "Missie May, you ain't eatin' yo' breakfus'."

90   "Ah don't choose none, Ah thank yuh."

91   His coffee cup was empty. She sprang to refill it. When she turned from the stove and bent to set the cup beside Joe's plate, she saw the yellow coin on the table between them.

92   She slumped into her seat and wept into her arms.

93   Presently Joe said calmly, "Missie May, you cry too much. Don't look back lak Lot's wife and turn to salt."

94   The sun, the hero of every day, the impersonal old man that beams as brightly on death as on birth, came up every morning and raced across the blue dome and dipped into the sea of fire every evening. Water ran down hill and birds nested.

95   Missie knew why she didn't leave Joe. She couldn't. She loved him too much. But she couldn't understand why Joe didn't leave her. He was polite, even kind at times, but aloof.

96   There were no more Saturday romps. No ringing silver dollars to stack beside her plate. No pockets to rifle. In fact the yellow coin in his trousers was like a monster hiding in the cave of his pockets to destroy her.

97   She often wondered if he still had it, but nothing could have induced her to ask nor yet to explore his pockets to see for herself. Its shadow was in the house whether or no.

98   One night Joe came home around midnight and complained of pains in the back. He asked Missie to rub him down with liniment. It had been three months since Missie had touched his body and it all seemed strange. But she rubbed him. Grateful for the chance. Before morning, youth triumphed and Missie exulted. But the next day, as she joyfully made up their bed, beneath her pillow she found the piece of money with the bit of chain attached.

99   Alone to herself, she looked at the thing with loathing, but look she must. She took it into the hands with trembling and saw first thing that it was no gold piece. It was a gilded half-dollar. Then she knew why Slemmons had forbidden anyone to touch his gold. He trusted village eyes at a distance not to recognize his stick-pin as a gilded quarter, and his watch charm as a four-bit piece.

100   She was glad at first that Joe had left it there. Perhaps he was through with her punishment. They were man and wife again. Then another thought came

NOTES

lak Lot's wife and turn to salt (par. 93): According to the Bible, Lot was told by God's angels to flee with his family to the hills in order to escape the destruction of Sodom and Gomorrah and not to look back. Lot's wife looked back and was turned into a pillar of salt (Genesis 19:12–26).

aloof (par. 95): distant

clawing at her. He had come home to buy from her as if she were any woman in the long house. Fifty cents for her love. As if to say that he could pay as well as Slemmons. She slid the coin into his Sunday pants pocket and dressed herself and left his house.

101   Halfway between her house and the quarters she met her husband's mother, and after a short talk she turned and went back home. If she had not the substance of marriage, she had the outside show. Joe must leave *her*. She let him see she didn't want his old gold four-bits too.

102   She saw no more of the coin for some time though she knew that Joe could not help finding it in his pocket. But his health kept poor, and he came home at least every ten days to be rubbed.

103   The sun swept around the horizon, trailing its robes of weeks and days. One morning as Joe came in from work, he found Missie May chopping wood. Without a word he took the ax and chopped a huge pile before he stopped.

104   "You ain't got no business choppin' wood, and you know it."

105   "How come? Ah been choppin' it for de last longest."

106   "Ah ain't blind. You makin' feet for shoes."

107   "Won't you be glad to have a li'l baby chile, Joe?"

108   "You know dat 'thout astin' me."

109   "Iss gointer be a boy chile and de very spit of you."

110   "You reckon, Missie May?"

111   "Who else could it look lak?"

112   Joe said nothing, but he thrust his hand deep into his pocket and fingered something there.

113   It was almost six months later Missie May took to bed and Joe went and got his mother to come wait on the house.

114   Missie May delivered a fine boy. Her travail was over when Joe came in from work one morning. His mother and the old women were drinking great bowls of coffee around the fire in the kitchen.

115   The minute Joe came into the room his mother called him aside.

116   "How did Missie May make out?" he asked quickly.

117   "Who, dat gal? She strong as a ox. She gointer have plenty mo'. We done fixed her wid de sugar and lard to sweeten her for de nex' one."

118   Joe stood silent awhile.

119   "You ain't ast 'bout de baby, Joe. You oughter be mighty proud cause he sho' is de spittin' image of yuh, son. Dat's yourn all right, if you never git another on, dat un is yourn. And you know Ah'm mighty proud too, son, cause Ah never thought well of you marryin' Missie May cause her make used tuh fan her foot 'round right smart and Ah been mighty skeered dat Missie May wuz gointer git misput on her road."

120   Joe said nothing. He fooled around the house till late in the day then just before he went to work, he went and stood at the foot of the bed and asked his wife how she felt. He did this every day during the week.

NOTES

de very spit of you (par. 109): the very spitting image of you: look just like you
travail (par. 114): labor (of childbirth)

121   On Saturday he went to Orlando to make his market. It had been a long time since he had done that.

122   Meat and lard, meal and flour, soap and starch. Cans of corn and tomatoes. All the staples. He fooled around town for a while and bought bananas and apples. Way after while he went around to the candy store.

123   "Hellow, Joe," the clerk greeted him. "Ain't seen you in a long time."

124   "Nope, Ah ain't been heah. Been 'round spots and places."

125   "Want some of them molasses kisses you always buy?"

126   "Yessuh." He threw the gilded half-dollar on the counter. "Will dat spend?"

127   "Whut is it, Joe? Well, I'll be doggone! A gold-plated four-bit piece. Where'd you git it, Joe?"

128   "Offen a stray nigger dat come through Eatonville. He had it on his watch chain for a charm—goin' 'round making out iss gold money. Ha ha! He had a quarter on his tie pin and it wuz all golded up too. Tryin' to fool people. Makin' out he is rich and everything. Ha! Ha! Tryin' to tole off folkses wives from home."

129   "How did you git it, Joe? Did he fool you, too?"

130   "Who, me? Naw suh! he ain't fooled me none. Know whut Ah done? He come 'round me wid his smart talk. Ah hauled off and knocked 'im down and took his old four-bits 'way from 'im. Gointer buy my wife some good ole 'lasses kisses wid it. Gimme fifty cents worth of dem candy kisses."

131   "Fifty cents buys a mighty lot of candy kisses, Joe. Why don't you split it up and take some chocolate bars, too. They eat good, too."

132   "Yessuh, dey do, but Ah wants all dat in kisses. Ah got a li'l boy chile home now. Tain't a week old yet, but he kin suck a sugar tit and maybe eat one them kisses hisself."

133   Joe got his candy and left the store. The clerk turned to the next customer. "Wisht I could be like these darkies. Laughin' all the time. Nothin' worries 'em."

134   Back in Eatonville, Joe reached his own front door. There was the ring of singing metal on wood. Fifteen times. Missie May couldn't run to the door, but she crept there as quickly as she could.

135   "Joe Banks, Ah hear you chunkin' money in mah do'way. You wait till Ah got mah strength back and Ah'm gointer fix you for dat."

Harrison Bergeron

Kurt Vonnegut, Jr.

1   The Year was 2081, and everybody was finally equal. They weren't only equal before God and the law. They were equal every which way. Nobody was smarter than anybody else. Nobody was better looking than anybody else. Nobody was stronger or quicker than anybody else. All this equality was due to the 211th, 212th, and 213th Amendments to the Constitution, and to the unceasing vigilance of agents of the United States Handicapper General.

NOTE

vigilance (par. 1): watchfulness

2   Some things about living still weren't quite right, though. April, for instance, still drove people crazy by not being springtime. And it was in that clammy month that the H-G men took George and Hazel Bergeron's fourteen-year-old son, Harrison, away.

3   It was tragic, all right, but George and Hazel couldn't think about it very hard. Hazel had a perfectly average intelligence, which meant she couldn't think about anything except in short bursts. And George, while his intelligence was way above normal, had a little mental handicap radio in his ear. He was required by law to wear it at all times. It was tuned to a government transmitter. Every twenty seconds or so, the transmitter would send out some sharp noise to keep people like George from taking unfair advantage of their brains.

4   George and Hazel were watching television. There were tears on Hazel's cheeks, but she'd forgotten for the moment what they were about.

5   On the television screen were ballerinas.

6   A buzzer sounded in George's head. His thoughts fled in panic, like bandits from a burglar alarm.

7   "That was a real pretty dance, that dance they just did," said Hazel.

8   "Huh," said George.

9   "That dance—it was nice," said Hazel.

10   "Yup," said George. He tried to think a little about the ballerinas. They weren't really very good—no better than anybody else would have been, anyway. They were burdened with sash weights and bags of birdshot, and their faces were masked, so that no one, seeing a free and graceful gesture or a pretty face, would feel like something the cat drug in. George was toying with the vague notion that maybe dancers shouldn't be handicapped. But he didn't get very far with it before another noise in his ear radio scattered his thoughts.

11   George winced. So did two out of the eight ballerinas.

12   Hazel saw him wince. Having no mental handicap herself, she had to ask George what the latest sound had been.

13   "Sounded like somebody hitting a milk bottle with a ball peen hammer," said George.

14   "I'd think it would be real interesting, hearing all the different sounds," said Hazel a little envious. "All the things they think up."

15   "Um," said George.

16   "Only, if I was Handicapper General, you know what I would do?" said Hazel. Hazel, as a matter of fact, bore a strong resemblance to the Handicapper General, a woman named Diana Moon Glampers. "If I was Diana Moon Glampers," said Hazel, "I'd have chimes on Sunday—just chimes. Kind of in honor of religion."

17   "I could think, if it was just chimes," said George.

18   "Well—maybe make 'em real loud," said Hazel. "I think I'd make a good Handicapper General."

19   "Good as anybody else," said George.

20   "Who knows better than I do what normal is?" said Hazel.

21   "Right," said George. He began to think glimmeringly about his abnormal son who was now in jail, about Harrison, but a twenty-one-gun salute in his head stopped that.

22   "Boy!" said Hazel, "that was a doozy, wasn't it?"

23   It was such a doozy that George was white and trembling, and tears stood on the rims of his red eyes. Two of the eight ballerinas had collapsed to the studio floor, were holding their temples.

24   "All of a sudden you look so tired," said Hazel. "Why don't you stretch out on the sofa, so's you can rest your handicap bag on the pillows, honeybunch." She was referring to the forty-seven pounds of birdshot in a canvas bag, which was padlocked around George's neck. "Go on and rest the bag for a little while," she said. "I don't care if you're not equal to me for a while."

25   George weighed the bag with his hands. "I don't mind it," he said. "I don't notice it any more. It's just a part of me."

26   "You been so tired lately—kind of wore out," said Hazel. "If there was just some way we could make a little hole in the bottom of the bag, and just take out a few of them lead balls. Just a few."

27   "Two years in prison and two thousand dollars fine for every ball I took out," said George. "I don't call that a bargain."

28   "If you could just take a few out when you came home from work," said Hazel. "I mean—you don't compete with anybody around here. You just set around."

29   "If I tried to get away with it," said George, "then other people'd get away with it—and pretty soon we'd be right back to the dark ages again, with everybody competing against everybody else. You wouldn't like that, would you?"

30   "I'd hate it," said Hazel.

31   "There you are," said George. "The minute people start cheating on laws, what do you think happens to society?"

32   If Hazel hadn't been able to come up with an answer to this question, George couldn't have supplied one. A siren was going off in his head.

33   "Reckon it'd fall all apart," said Hazel.

34   "What would?" said George blankly.

35   "Society," said Hazel uncertainly. "Wasn't that what you just said?"

36   "Who knows?" said George.

37   The television program was suddenly interrupted for a news bulletin. It wasn't clear at first as to what the bulletin was about, since the announcer, like all announcers, had a serious speech impediment. For about half a minute, and in a state of high excitement, the announcer tried to say, "Ladies and Gentlemen."

38   He finally gave up, handed the bulletin to a ballerina to read.

39   "That's all right—" Hazel said of the announcer, "he tried. That's the big thing. He tried to do the best he could with what God gave him. He should get a nice raise for trying so hard."

40   "Ladies and Gentlemen," said the ballerina, reading the bulletin. She must have been extraordinarily beautiful, because the mask she wore was hideous. And it was easy to see that she was the strongest and most graceful of all the dancers, for her handicap bags were as big as those worn by two-hundred pound men.

41   And she had to apologize at once for her voice, which was a very unfair voice for a woman to use. Her voice was a warm, luminous, timeless melody. "Excuse me—" she said, and she began again, making her voice absolutely uncompetitive.

NOTE

luminous (par. 41): clear; easily understood

42   "Harrison Bergeron, age fourteen," she said in a grackle squawk, "has just escaped from jail, where he was held on suspicion of plotting to overthrow the government. He is a genius and an athlete, is under-handicapped, and should be regarded as extremely dangerous."

43   A police photograph of Harrison Bergeron was flashed on the screen—upside down, then sideways, upside down again, then right side up. The picture showed the full length of Harrison against a background calibrated in feet and inches. He was exactly seven feet tall.

44   The rest of Harrison's appearance was Halloween and hardware. Nobody had ever borne heavier handicaps. He had outgrown hindrances faster than the H-G men could think them up. Instead of a little ear radio for a mental handicap, he wore a tremendous pair of earphones, and spectacles with thick wavy lenses. The spectacles were intended to make him not only half blind, but to give him whanging headaches besides.

45   Scrap metal was hung all over him. Ordinarily, there was a certain symmetry, a military neatness to the handicaps issued to strong people, but Harrison looked like a walking junkyard. In the race of life, Harrison carried three hundred pounds.

46   And to offset his good looks, the H-G men required that he wear at all times a red rubber ball for a nose, keep his eyebrows shaved off, and cover his even white teeth with black caps at snaggle-tooth random.

47   "If you see this boy," said the ballerina, "do not—I repeat, do not—try to reason with him."

48   There was the shriek of a door being torn from its hinges.

49   Screams and barking cries of consternation came from the television set. The photograph of Harrison Bergeron on the screen jumped again and again, as though dancing to the tune of an earthquake.

50   George Bergeron correctly identified the earthquake, and well he might have—for many was the time his own home had danced to the same crashing tune. "My God—" said George, "that must be Harrison!"

51   The realization was blasted from his mind instantly by the sound of an automobile collision in his head.

52   When George could open his eyes again, the photograph of Harrison was gone. A living, breathing Harrison filled the screen.

53   Clanking, clownish, and huge, Harrison stood in the center of the studio. The knob of the uprooted studio door was still in his hand. Ballerinas, technicians, musicians, and announcers cowered on their knees before him, expecting to die.

54   "I am the Emperor!" cried Harrison. "Do you hear? I am the Emperor! Everybody must do what I say at once!" He stamped his foot and the studio shook.

55   "Even as I stand here" he bellowed, "crippled, hobbled, sickened—I am a greater ruler than any man who ever lived! Now watch me become what I can become!"

56   Harrison tore the straps of his handicap harness like wet tissue paper, tore straps guaranteed to support five thousand pounds.

NOTES

calibrated (par. 43): marked
consternation (par. 49): fear
cowered (par. 53): crouched

57   Harrison's scrap-iron handicaps crashed to the floor.

58   Harrison thrust his thumbs under the bar of the padlock that secured his head harness. The bar snapped like celery. Harrison smashed his headphones and spectacles against the wall.

59   He flung away his rubber-ball nose, revealed a man that would have awed Thor, the god of thunder.

60   "I shall now select my Empress!" he said, looking down on the cowering people. "Let the first woman who dares rise to her feet claim her mate and her throne!"

61   A moment passed, and then a ballerina arose, swaying like a willow.

62   Harrison plucked the mental handicap from her ear, snapped off her physical handicaps with marvelous delicacy. Last of all he removed her mask.

63   She was blindingly beautiful.

64   "Now—" said Harrison, taking her hand, "shall we show the people the meaning of the word dance? Music!" he commanded.

65   The musicians scrambled back into their chairs, and Harrison stripped them of their handicaps, too. "Play your best," he told them, "and I'll make you barons and dukes and earls."

66   The music began. It was normal at first—cheap, silly, false. But Harrison snatched two musicians from their chairs, waved them like batons as he sang the music as he wanted it played. He slammed them back into their chairs.

67   The music began again and was much improved.

68   Harrison and his Empress merely listened to the music for a while— listened gravely, as though synchronizing their heartbeats with it.

69   They shifted their weights to their toes.

70   Harrison placed his big hands on the girl's tiny waist, letting her sense the weightlessness that would soon be hers.

71   And then, in an explosion of joy and grace, into the air they sprang!

72   Not only were the laws of the land abandoned, but the law of gravity and the laws of motion as well.

73   They reeled, whirled, swiveled, flounced, capered, gamboled, and spun.

74   They leaped like deer on the moon.

75   The studio ceiling was thirty feet high, but each leap brought the dancers nearer to it.

76   It became their obvious intention to kiss the ceiling. They kissed it.

77   And then, neutralizing gravity with love and pure will, they remained suspended in air inches below the ceiling, and they kissed each other for a long, long time.

78   It was then that Diana Moon Glampers, the Handicapper General, came into the studio with a double-barreled ten-gauge shotgun. She fired twice, and the Emperor and the Empress were dead before they hit the floor.

79   Diana Moon Glampers loaded the gun again. She aimed it at the musicians and told them they had ten seconds to get their handicaps back on.

80   It was then that the Bergerons' television tube burned out.

81   Hazel turned to comment about the blackout to George. But George had gone out into the kitchen for a can of beer.

82   George came back in with the beer, paused while a handicap signal shook him up. And then he sat down again. "You been crying" he said to Hazel.

83   "Yup," she said.

84   "What about?" he said.

85   "I forget," she said. "Something real sad on television."

86   "What was it?" he said.

87   "It's all kind of mixed up in my mind," said Hazel.

88   "Forget sad things," said George.

89   "I always do," said Hazel.

90   "That's my girl," said George. He winced. There was the sound of a riveting gun in his head.

91   "Gee—I could tell that one was a doozy," said Hazel.

92   "You can say that again," said George.

93   "Gee—" said Hazel, "I could tell that one was a doozy."

The Fat Girl

Andre Dubus

1   Her name was Louise. Once when she was sixteen a boy kissed her at a barbecue; he was drunk and he jammed his tongue into her mouth and ran his hands up and down her hips. Her father kissed her often. He was thin and kind and she could see in his eyes when he looked at her the lights of love and pity.

2   It started when Louise was nine. You must start watching what you eat, her mother would say. I can see you have my metabolism. Louise also had her mother's pale blonde hair. Her mother was slim and pretty, carried herself erectly, and ate very little. The two of them would eat bare lunches, while her older brother ate sandwiches and potato chips, and then her mother would sit smoking while Louise eyed the bread box, the pantry, the refrigerator. Wasn't that good, her mother would say. In five years you'll be in high school and if you're fat the boys won't like you; they won't ask you out. Boys were as far away as five years, and she would go to her room and wait for nearly an hour until she knew her mother was no longer thinking of her, then she would creep into the kitchen and, listening to her mother talking on the phone, or her footsteps upstairs, she would open the bread box, the pantry, the jar of peanut butter. She would put the sandwich under her shirt and go outside or to the bathroom to eat it.

3   Her father was a lawyer and made a lot of money and came home looking pale and happy. Martinis put color back in his face, and at dinner he talked to his wife and two children. Oh give her a potato, he would say to Louise's mother. She's a growing girl. Her mother's voice then became tense: If she has a potato she shouldn't have dessert. She should have both, her father would say, and he would reach over and touch Louise's cheek or hand or arm.

4   In high school she had two girl friends and at night and on weekends they rode in a car or went to movies. In movies she was fascinated by fat actresses. She wondered why they were fat. She knew why she was fat: she was

NOTE

metabolism (par. 2): the chemical process through which the body breaks down and uses food

fat because she was Louise. Because God had made her that way. Because she wasn't like her friends Joan and Marjorie, who drank milk shakes after school and were all bones and tight skin. But what about those actresses, with their talents, with their broad and profound faces? Did they eat as heedlessly as Bishop Humphries and his wife who sometimes came to dinner and, as Louise's mother said, gorged between amenities? Or did they try to lose weight, did they go about hungry and angry and thinking of food? She thought of them eating lean meats and salads with friends, and then going home and building strange large sandwiches with French bread. But mostly she believed they did not go through these failures; they were fat because they chose to be. And she was certain of something else too: she could see it in their faces: they did not eat secretly. Which she did: her creeping to the kitchen when she was nine became, in high school, a ritual of deceit and pleasure. She was a furtive eater of sweets. Even her two friends did not know her secret.

5   Joan was thin, gangling, and flat-chested; she was attractive enough and all she needed was someone to take a second look at her face, but the school was large and there were pretty girls in every classroom and walking all the corridors, so no one ever needed to take a second look at Joan. Marjorie was thin too, an intense, heavy-smoking girl with brittle laughter. She was very intelligent, and with boys she was shy because she knew she made them uncomfortable, and because she was smarter than they were and so could not understand or could not believe the levels they lived on. She was to have a nervous breakdown before earning her Ph.D. in philosophy at the University of California, where she met and married a physicist and discovered within herself an untrammelled passion: she made love with her husband on the couch, the carpet, in the bathtub, and on the washing machine. By that time much had happened to her and she never thought of Louise. Joan would finally stop growing and begin moving with grace and confidence. In college she would have two lovers and then several more during the six years she spent in Boston before marrying a middle-aged editor who had two sons in their early teens, who drank too much, who was tenderly, boyishly grateful for her love, and whose wife had been killed while rock climbing in New Hampshire with her lover. She would not think of Louise either, except in an earlier time, when lovers were still new to her and she was ecstatically surprised each time one of them loved her and, sometimes at night, lying in a man's arms, she would tell how in high school no one dated her, she had been thin and plain (she would still believe that: that she had been plain; it had never been true) and so had been forced into the weekend and nighttime company of a neurotic smart girl and a shy fat girl. She would say this with self-pity exaggerated by Scotch and her need to be more deeply loved by the man who held her.

NOTES

heedlessly (par. 4): unconcerned
gorged (par. 4): stuffed themselves
amenities (par. 4): polite conversations
furtive (par. 4): secret
gangling (par. 5): tall and awkward
untrammelled (par. 5): unrestricted
ecstatically (par. 5): overwhelmingly, joyfully

6   She never eats, Joan and Marjorie said of Louise. They ate lunch with her at school, watched her refusing potatoes, ravioli, fried fish. Sometimes she got through the cafeteria line with only a salad. That is how they would remember her: a girl whose hapless body was destined to be fat. No one saw the sandwiches she made and took to her room when she came home from school. No one saw the store of Milky Ways, Butterfingers, Almond Joys, and Hersheys far back on her closet shelf, behind the stuffed animals of her childhood. She was not a hypocrite. When she was out of the house she truly believed she was dieting; she forgot about the candy, as a man speaking into his office dictaphone may forget the lewd photographs hidden in an old shoe in his closet. At other times, away from home, she thought of the waiting candy with near lust. One night driving home from a movie, Marjorie said: "You're lucky you don't smoke; it's incredible what I go through to hide it from my parents." Louise turned to her a smile which was elusive and mysterious; she yearned to be home in bed, eating chocolate in the dark. She did not need to smoke; she already had a vice that was insular and destructive.

7   She brought it with her to college. She thought she would leave it behind. A move from one place to another, a new room without the haunted closet shelf, would do for her what she could not do for herself. She packed her large dresses and went. For two weeks she was busy with registration, with shyness, with classes; then she began to feel at home. Her room was no longer like a motel. Its walls had stopped watching her, she felt they were her friends, and she gave them her secret. Away from her mother, she did not have to be as elaborate; she kept the candy in her drawer now.

8   The school was in Massachusetts, a girls' school. When she chose it, when she and her father and mother talked about it in the evenings, everyone so carefully avoided the word boys that sometimes the conversations seemed to be about nothing but boys. There are no boys there, the neuter words said; you will not have to contend with that. In her father's eyes were pity and encouragement; in her mother's was disappointment, and her voice was crisp. They spoke of courses, of small classes where Louise would get more attention. She imagined herself in those small classes; she saw herself as a teacher would see her, as the other girls would; she would get no attention.

9   The girls at the school were from wealthy families, but most of them wore the uniform of another class: blue jeans and work shirts, and many wore overalls. Louise bought some overalls, washed them until the dark blue faded, and wore them to classes. In the cafeteria she ate as she had in high school, not to lose weight nor even to sustain her lie, but because eating lightly in public

NOTES

hapless (par. 6): unfortunate
hypocrite (par. 6): a person who says one thing and does the opposite
lewd (par. 6): obscene
elusive (par. 6): deceptive
insular (par. 6): concealed
elaborate (par. 7): careful
neuter (par. 8): literally, having neither male nor female characteristics
sustain (par. 9): maintain

had become as habitual as good manners. Everyone had to take gym, and in the locker room with the other girls, and wearing shorts on the volleyball and badminton courts, she hated her body. She liked her body most when she was unaware of it: in bed at night, as sleep gently took her out of her day, out of herself. And she liked parts of her body. She liked her brown eyes and sometimes looked at them in the mirror: they were not shallow eyes, she thought; they were indeed windows of a tender soul, a good heart. She liked her lips and nose, and her chin, finely shaped between her wide and sagging cheeks. Most of all she liked her long pale blonde hair, she liked washing and drying it and lying naked on her bed, smelling of shampoo, and feeling the soft hair at her neck and shoulders and back.

10   Her friend at college was Carrie, who was thin and wore thick glasses and often at night she cried in Louise's room. She did not know why she was crying. She was crying, she said, because she was unhappy. She could say no more. Louise said she was unhappy too, and Carrie moved in with her. One night Carrie talked for hours, sadly and bitterly, about her parents and what they did to each other. When she finished she hugged Louise and they went to bed. Then in the dark Carrie spoke across the room: "Louise? I just wanted to tell you. One night last week I woke up and smelled chocolate. You were eating chocolate, in your bed. I wish you'd eat it in front of me, Louise, whenever you feel like it."

11   Stiffened in her bed, Louise could think of nothing to say. In the silence she was afraid Carrie would think she was asleep and would tell her again in the morning or tomorrow night. Finally she said Okay. Then after a moment she told Carrie if she ever wanted any she could feel free to help herself; the candy was in the top drawer. Then she said "Thank you."

12   They were roommates for four years and in the summers they exchanged letters. Each fall they greeted with embraces, laughter, tears, and moved into their old room, which had been stripped and cleansed of them for the summer. Neither girl enjoyed summer. Carrie did not like being at home because her parents did not love each other. Louise lived in a small city in Louisiana. She did not like summer because she had lost touch with Joan and Marjorie; they saw each other, but it was not the same. She liked being with her father but with no one else. The flicker of disappointment in her mother's eyes at the airport was a vanguard of the army of relatives and acquaintances who awaited her: they would see her on the streets, in stores, at the country club, in her home, and in theirs; in the first moments of greeting, their eyes would tell her she was still fat Louise, who had been fat as long as they could remember, who had gone to college and returned as fat as ever. Then their eyes dismissed her, and she longed for school and Carrie, and she wrote letters to her friend. But that saddened her too. It wasn't simply that Carrie was her only friend, and when they finished college they might never see each other again. It was that her existence in the world was so divided; it had begun when she was a child creeping to the kitchen; now that division was much sharper, and her

NOTE

vanguard (par. 12): literally, the troops at the head of an army

friendship with Carrie seemed disproportionate and perilous. The world she was destined to live in had nothing to do with the intimate nights in their room at school.

13   In the summer before their senior year, Carrie fell in love. She wrote to Louise about him, but she did not write much, and this hurt Louise more than if Carrie had shown the joy her writing tried to conceal. That fall they returned to their room; they were still close and warm, Carrie still needed Louise's ears and heart at night as she spoke of her parents and her recurring malaise whose source the two friends never discovered. But on most weekends Carrie left, and caught a bus to Boston where her boyfriend studied music. During the week she often spoke hesitantly of sex; she was not sure if she liked it. But Louise, eating candy and listening, did not know whether Carrie was telling the truth or whether, as in her letters of the past summer, Carrie was keeping from her those delights she may never experience.

14   Then one Sunday night when Carrie had just returned from Boston and was unpacking her overnight bag, she looked at Louise and said: "I was thinking about you. On the bus coming home tonight." Looking at Carrie's concerned, determined face, Louise prepared herself for humiliation. "I was thinking about when we graduate. What you're going to do. What's to become of you. I want you to be loved the way I love you. Louise, if I help you, *really* help you, will you go on a diet?"

15   Louise entered a period of her life she would remember always, the way some people remember having endured poverty. Her diet did not begin the next day. Carrie told her to eat on Monday as though it were the last day of her life. So for the first time since grammar school Louise went into a school cafeteria and ate everything she wanted. At breakfast and lunch and dinner she glanced around the table to see if the other girls noticed the food on her tray. They did not. She felt there was a lesson in this, but it lay beyond her grasp. That night in their room she ate the four remaining candy bars. During the day Carrie rented a small refrigerator, bought an electric skillet, an electric broiler, and bathroom scales.

16   On Tuesday morning Louise stood on the scales, and Carrie wrote in her notebook: *October 14: 184 lbs.* Then she made Louise a cup of black coffee and scrambled one egg and sat with her while she ate. When Carrie went to the dining room for breakfast, Louise walked about the campus for thirty minutes. That was part of the plan. The campus was pretty, on its lawns grew at least one of every tree native to New England, and in the warm morning sun Louise felt a new hope. At noon they met in their room, and Carrie broiled her a piece of hamburger and served it with lettuce. Then while Carrie ate in the dining room Louise walked again. She was weak with hunger and she felt queasy. During her afternoon classes she was nervous and tense and

NOTES

perilous (par. 12): risky
destined (par. 12): certain
intimate (par. 12): very personal
malaise (par. 13): depression
queasy (par. 16): nauseated

she chewed her pencil and tapped her heels on the floor and tightened her calves. When she returned to her room late that afternoon, she was so glad to see Carrie that she embraced her; she had felt she could not bear another minute of hunger, but now with Carrie she knew she could make it at least through tonight. Then she would sleep and face tomorrow when it came. Carrie broiled her a steak and served it with lettuce. Louise studied while Carrie ate dinner, then they went for a walk.

17   That was her ritual and her diet for the rest of the year, Carrie alternating fish and chicken breasts with the steaks for dinner, and every day was nearly as bad as the first. In the evenings she was irritable. In all her life she had never been afflicted by ill temper and she looked upon it now as a demon which, along with hunger, was taking possession of her soul. Often she spoke sharply to Carrie. One night during their after-dinner walk Carrie talked sadly of night, of how darkness made her more aware of herself, and at night she did not know why she was in college, why she studied, why she was walking the earth with other people. They were standing on a wooden foot bridge looking down at a dark pond. Carrie kept talking; perhaps soon she would cry. Suddenly Louise said: "I'm sick of lettuce. I never want to see a piece of lettuce for the rest of my life. I hate it. We shouldn't even buy it, it's immoral."

18   Carrie was quiet. Louise glanced at her, and the pain and irritation in Carrie's face soothed her. Then she was ashamed. Before she could say she was sorry, Carrie turned to her and said gently: "I know. I know how terrible it is."

19   Carrie did all the shopping, telling Louise she knew how hard it was to go into a supermarket when you were hungry. And Louise was always hungry. She drank diet soft drinks and started smoking Carrie's cigarettes, learned to enjoy inhaling, thought of cancer and emphysema but they were as far away as those boys her mother had talked about when she was nine. By Thanksgiving she was smoking over a pack a day and her weight in Carrie's notebook was one hundred and sixty-two pounds. Carrie was afraid if Louise went home at Thanksgiving she would lapse from the diet, so Louise spent the vacation with Carrie, in Philadelphia. Carrie wrote her family about the diet, and told Louise that she had. On the phone to Philadelphia, Louise said: "I feel like a bedwetter. When I was a little girl I had a friend who used to come spend the night and Mother would put a rubber sheet on the bed and we all pretended there wasn't a rubber sheet and that she hadn't wet the bed. Even me, and I slept with her." At Thanksgiving dinner she lowered her eyes as Carrie's father put two slices of white meat on her plate and passed it to her over the bowls of steaming food.

20   When she went home at Christmas she weighed a hundred and fifty-five pounds; at the airport her mother marvelled. Her father laughed and hugged her and said: "But now there's less of you to love." He was troubled by her smoking but only mentioned it once; he told her she was beautiful and, as always, his eyes bathed her with love. During the long vacation her mother

NOTE

afflicted (par. 17): troubled

cooked for her as Carrie had, and Louise returned to school weighing a hundred and forty-six pounds.

21   Flying north on the plane she warmly recalled the surprised and congratulatory eyes of her relatives and acquaintances. She had not seen Joan or Marjorie. She thought of returning home in May, weighing the hundred and fifteen pounds which Carrie had in October set as their goal. Looking toward the stoic days ahead, she felt strong. She thought of those hungry days of fall and early winter (and now: she was hungry now: with almost a frown, almost a brusque shake of the head, she refused peanuts from the stewardess): those first weeks of the diet when she was the pawn of an irascibility which still, conditioned to her ritual as she was, could at any moment take command of her. She thought of the nights of trying to sleep while her stomach growled. She thought of her addiction to cigarettes. She thought of the people at school: not one teacher, not one girl, had spoken to her about her loss of weight, not even about her absence from meals. And without warning her spirit collapsed. She did not feel strong, she did not feel she was committed to and within reach of achieving a valuable goal. She felt that somehow she had lost more than pounds of fat; that some time during her dieting she had lost herself too. She tried to remember what it had felt like to be Louise before she had started living on meat and fish, as an unhappy adult may look sadly in the memory of childhood for lost virtues and hopes. She looked down at the earth far below, and it seemed to her that her soul, like her body aboard the plane, was in some rootless flight. She neither knew its destination or where it had departed from; it was on some passage she could not even define.

22   During the next few weeks she lost weight more slowly and once for eight days Carrie's daily recording stayed at a hundred and thirty-six. Louise woke in the morning thinking of one hundred and thirty-six and then she stood on the scales and they echoed her. She became obsessed with that number, and there wasn't a day when she didn't say it aloud, and through the days and nights the number stayed in her mind, and if a teacher had spoken those digits in a classroom she would have opened her mouth to speak. What if that's me, she said to Carrie. I mean what if a hundred and thirty-six is my real weight and I just can't lose anymore. Walking hand-in-hand with her despair was a longing for this to be true, and that longing angered her and wearied her, and every day she was gloomy. On the ninth day she weighed a hundred and thirty-five and a half pounds. She was not relieved; she thought bitterly of the months ahead, the shedding of the last twenty and a half pounds.

23   On Easter Sunday, which she spent at Carrie's, she weighed one hundred and twenty pounds, and she ate one slice of glazed pineapple with her ham and lettuce. She did not enjoy it: she felt she was being friendly with a recalcitrant enemy who had once tried to destroy her. Carrie's parents were

NOTES

stoic (par. 21): literally, showing no reaction to pleasure or pain

brusque (par. 21): abrupt, rude

pawn (par. 21): literally, one who is controlled by another

irascibility (par. 21): anger, irritability

recalcitrant (par. 23): difficult to control or overcome

1 P.M.

48   Rose of Sharon, Junior, and I carried our twenty-dollar bill and our five dollars in loose change over to the 7-Eleven and bought three bottles of imagination. We needed to figure out how to raise all that money in only one day. Thinking hard, we huddled in an alley beneath the Alaska Way Viaduct and finished off those bottles—one, two, and three.

2 P.M.

49   Rose of Sharon was gone when I woke up. I heard later that she had hitch-hiked back to Toppenish and was living with her sister on the reservation.

50   Junior had passed out beside me and was covered in his own vomit, or maybe somebody else's vomit, and my head hurt from thinking, so I left him alone and walked down to the water. I love the smell of ocean water. Salt always smells like memory.

51   When I got to the wharf, I ran into three Aleut cousins, who sat on a wooden bench and stared out at the bay and cried. Most of the homeless Indians in Seattle come from Alaska. One by one, each of them hopped a big working boat in Anchorage or Barrow or Juneau, fished his way south to Seattle, jumped off the boat with a pocketful of cash to party hard at one of the highly sacred and traditional Indian bars, went broke and broker, and has been trying to find his way back to the boat and the frozen North ever since.

52   These Aleuts smelled like salmon, I thought, and they told me they were going to sit on that wooden bench until their boat came back.

53   "How long has your boat been gone?" I asked.

54   "Eleven years," the elder Aleut said.

55   I cried with them for a while.

56   "Hey," I said. "Do you guys have any money I can borrow?"

57   They didn't.

3 P.M.

58   I walked back to Junior. He was still out cold. I put my face down near his mouth to make sure he was breathing. He was alive, so I dug around in his blue jeans pockets and found half a cigarette. I smoked it all the way down and thought about my grandmother.

59   Her name was Agnes, and she died of breast cancer when I was fourteen. My father always thought Agnes caught her tumors from the uranium mine on the reservation. But my mother said the disease started when Agnes was walking back from a pow-wow one night and got run over by a motorcycle. She broke three ribs, and my mother always said those ribs never healed right, and tumors take over when you don't heal right.

NOTES

Viaduct (par. 48): bridge
Toppenish (par. 49): a tourist town located on the Yakima Indian Reservation
Aleut (par. 51): Native Americans inhabiting the Aleutian Islands and coastal areas of southwestern Alaska
uranium (par. 59): a radioactive and poisonous element occurring in several minerals and used for nuclear fuel and nuclear weapons

60   Sitting beside Junior, smelling the smoke and the salt and the vomit, I wondered if my grandmother's cancer started when somebody stole her pow-wow regalia. Maybe the cancer started in her broken heart and then leaked out into her breasts. I know it's crazy, but I wondered whether I could bring my grandmother back to life if I bought back her regalia.

61   I needed money, big money, so I left Junior and walked over to the Real Change office.

4 P.M.

62   Real Change is a multifaceted organization that publishes a newspaper, supports cultural projects that empower the poor and the homeless, and mobilizes the public around poverty issues. Real Change's mission is to organize, educate, and build alliances to create solutions to homelessness and poverty. It exists to provide a voice for poor people in our community.

63   I memorized Real Change's mission statement because I sometimes sell the newspaper on the streets. But you have to stay sober to sell it, and I'm not always good at staying sober. Anybody can sell the paper. You buy each copy for thirty cents and sell it for a dollar, and you keep the profit.

64   "I need one thousand four hundred and thirty papers," I said to the Big Boss.

65   "That's a strange number," he said. "And that's a lot of papers."

66   "I need them."

67   The Big Boss pulled out his calculator and did the math.

68   "It will cost you four hundred and twenty-nine dollars for that many," he said.

69   "If I had that kind of money, I wouldn't need to sell the papers."

70   "What's going on, Jackson-to-the-Second-Power?" he asked. He is the only person who calls me that. He's a funny and kind man.

71   I told him about my grandmother's pow-wow regalia and how much money I needed in order to buy it back.

72   "We should call the police," he said.

73   "I don't want to do that," I said. "It's a quest now. I need to win it back by myself."

74   "I understand," he said. "And, to be honest, I'd give you the papers to sell if I thought it would work. But the record for the most papers sold in one day by one vender is only three hundred and two."

75   "That would net me about two hundred bucks," I said.

76   The Big Boss used his calculator. "Two hundred and eleven dollars and forty cents," he said.

77   "That's not enough," I said.

78   "And the most money anybody has made in one day is five hundred and twenty-five. And that's because somebody gave Old Blue five hundred-dollar bills for some dang reason. The average daily net is about thirty dollars."

NOTES

alliances (par. 62): partnerships
quest (par. 73): search

79   "This isn't going to work."

80   "No."

81   "Can you lend me some money?"

82   "I can't do that," he said. "If I lend you money, I have to lend money to everybody."

83   "What can you do?"

84   "I'll give you fifty papers for free. But don't tell anybody I did it."

85   "O.K.," I said.

86   He gathered up the newspapers and handed them to me. I held them to my chest. He hugged me. I carried the newspapers back toward the water.

5 P.M.

87   Back on the wharf, I stood near the Bainbridge Island Terminal and tried to sell papers to business commuters boarding the ferry.

88   I sold five in one hour, dumped the other forty-five in a garbage can, and walked into McDonald's, ordered four cheeseburgers for a dollar each, and slowly ate them.

89   After eating, I walked outside and vomited on the sidewalk. I hated to lose my food so soon after eating it. As an alcoholic Indian with a busted stomach, I always hope I can keep enough food in me to stay alive.

6 P.M.

90   With one dollar in my pocket, I walked back to Junior. He was still passed out, and I put my ear to his chest and listened for his heartbeat. He was alive, so I took off his shoes and socks and found one dollar in his left sock and fifty cents in his right sock.

91   With two dollars and fifty cents in my hand, I sat beside Junior and thought about my grandmother and her stories.

92   When I was thirteen, my grandmother told me a story about the Second World War. She was a nurse at a military hospital in Sydney, Australia. For two years, she healed and comforted American and Australian soldiers.

93   One day, she tended to a wounded Maori soldier, who had lost his legs to an artillery attack. He was very dark-skinned. His hair was black and curly and his eyes were black and warm. His face was covered with bright tattoos.

94   "Are you Maori?" he asked my grandmother.

95   "No," she said. "I'm Spokane Indian. From the United States."

96   "Ah, yes," he said. "I have heard of your tribes. But you are the first American Indian I have ever met."

97   "There's a lot of Indian soldiers fighting for the United States," she said. "I have a brother fighting in Germany, and I lost another brother on Okinawa."

98   "I am sorry," he said. "I was on Okinawa as well. It was terrible."

99   "I am sorry about your legs," my grandmother said.

100   "It's funny, isn't it?" he said.

101   "What's funny?"

NOTE

Maori (par. 93): Polynesian people native to New Zealand

102   "How we brown people are killing other brown people so white people will remain free."

103   "I hadn't thought of it that way."

104   "Well, sometimes I think of it that way. And other times I think of it the way they want me to think of it. I get confused."

105   She fed him morphine.

106   "Do you believe in Heaven?" he asked.

107   "Which Heaven?" she asked.

108   "I'm talking about the Heaven where my legs are waiting for me."

109   They laughed.

110   "Of course," he said, "my legs will probably run away from me when I get to Heaven. And how will I ever catch them?"

111   "You have to get your arms strong," my grandmother said. "So you can run on your hands."

112   They laughed again.

113   Sitting beside Junior, I laughed at the memory of my grandmother's story. I put my hand close to Junior's mouth to make sure he was still breathing. Yes, Junior was alive, so I took my two dollars and fifty cents and walked to the Korean grocery store in Pioneer Square.

7 P.M.

114   At the Korean grocery store, I bought a fifty-cent cigar and two scratch lottery tickets for a dollar each. The maximum cash prize was five hundred dollars a ticket. If I won both, I would have enough money to buy back the regalia.

115   I loved Mary, the young Korean woman who worked the register. She was the daughter of the owners, and she sang all day.

116   "I love you," I said when I handed her the money.

117   "You always say you love me," she said.

118   "That's because I will always love you."

119   "You are a sentimental fool."

120   "I'm a romantic old man."

121   "Too old for me."

122   "I know I'm too old for you, but I can dream."

123   "O.K.," she said. "I agree to be a part of your dreams, but I will only hold your hand in your dreams. No kissing and no sex. Not even in your dreams."

124   "O.K.," I said. "No sex. Just romance."

125   "Goodbye, Jackson Jackson, my love. I will see you soon."

126   I left the store, walked over to Occidental Park, sat on a bench, and smoked my cigar all the way down.

127   Ten minutes after I finished the cigar, I scratched my first lottery ticket and won nothing. I could only win five hundred dollars now, and that would only be half of what I needed.

128   Ten minutes after I lost, I scratched the other ticket and won a free ticket— a small consolation and one more chance to win some money.

129   I walked back to Mary.

130   "Jackson Jackson," she said. "Have you come back to claim my heart?"

131   "I won a free ticket," I said.

132   "Just like a man," she said. "You love money and power more than you love me."

133   "It's true," I said. "And I'm sorry it's true."

134   She gave me another scratch ticket, and I took it outside. I like to scratch my tickets in private. Hopeful and sad, I scratched that third ticket and won real money. I carried it back inside to Mary.

135   "I won a hundred dollars," I said.

136   She examined the ticket and laughed.

137   "That's a fortune," she said, and counted out five twenties. Our fingertips touched as she handed me the money. I felt electric and constant.

138   "Thank you," I said, and gave her one of the bills.

139   "I can't take that," she said. "It's your money."

140   "No, it's tribal. It's an Indian thing. When you win, you're supposed to share with your family."

141   "I'm not your family."

142   "Yes, you are."

143   She smiled. She kept the money. With eighty dollars in my pocket, I said goodbye to my dear Mary and walked out into the cold night air.

8 P.M.

144   I wanted to share the good news with Junior. I walked back to him, but he was gone. I heard later that he had hitchhiked down to Portland, Oregon, and died of exposure in an alley behind the Hilton Hotel.

9 P.M.

145   Lonesome for Indians, I carried my eighty dollars over to Big Heart's in South Downtown. Big Heart's is an all-Indian bar. Nobody knows how or why Indians migrate to one bar and turn it into an official Indian bar. But Big Heart's has been an Indian bar for twenty-three years. It used to be way up on Aurora Avenue, but a crazy Lummi Indian burned that one down, and the owners moved to the new location, a few blocks south of Safeco Field.

146   I walked into Big Heart's and counted fifteen Indians—eight men and seven women. I didn't know any of them, but Indians like to belong, so we all pretended to be cousins.

147   "How much for whiskey shots?" I asked the bartender, a fat white guy.

148   "You want the bad stuff or the badder stuff?"

149   "As bad as you got."

150   "One dollar a shot."

151   I laid my eighty dollars on the bar top.

152   "All right," I said. "Me and all my cousins here are going to be drinking eighty shots. How many is that apiece?"

153   "Counting you," a woman shouted from behind me, "that's five shots for everybody."

NOTES

migrate (par. 145): move to

Lummi (par. 145): Native American tribe from the west coast of Washington

their thighs, spinning with slow motes in the single sun-ray. On a tarnished gilt easel before the fireplace stood a crayon portrait of Miss Emily's father.

6   They rose when she entered—a small, fat woman in black, with a thin gold chain descending to her waist and vanishing into her belt, leaning on an ebony cane with a tarnished gold head. Her skeleton was small and spare; perhaps that was why what would have been merely plumpness in another was obesity in her. She looked bloated, like a body long submerged in motionless water, and of that pallid hue. Her eyes, lost in the fatty ridges of her face, looked like two small pieces of coal pressed into a lump of dough as they moved from one face to another while the visitors stated their errand.

7   She did not ask them to sit. She just stood in the door and listened quietly until the spokesman came to a stumbling halt. Then they could hear the invisible watch ticking at the end of the gold chain.

8   Her voice was dry and cold. "I have no taxes in Jefferson. Colonel Sartoris explained it to me. Perhaps one of you can gain access to the city records and satisfy yourselves."

9   "But we have. We are the city authorities, Miss Emily. Didn't you get a notice from the sheriff, signed by him?"

10   "I received a paper, yes," Miss Emily said. "Perhaps he considers himself the sheriff . . . I have no taxes in Jefferson."

11   "But there is nothing on the books to show that, you see. We must go by the—"

12   "See Colonel Sartoris. I have no taxes in Jefferson."

13   "But, Miss Emily—"

14   "See Colonel Sartoris." (Colonel Sartoris had been dead almost ten years.) "I have no taxes in Jefferson. Tobe!" The Negro appeared. "Show these gentlemen out."

II

15   So she vanquished them, horse and foot, just as she had vanquished their fathers thirty years before about the smell. That was two years after her father's death and a short time after her sweetheart—the one we believed would marry her—had deserted her. After her father's death she went out very little; after her sweetheart went away, people hardly saw her at all. A few of the ladies had the temerity to call, but were not received, and the only sign of life about the place was the Negro man—a young man then—going in and out with a market basket.

16   "Just as if a man—any man—could keep a kitchen properly," the ladies said; so they were not surprised when the smell developed. It was another link between the gross, teeming world and the high and mighty Griersons.

NOTES

motes (par. 5): specks
gilt (par. 5): a gold coating
ebony (par. 6): a black wood
pallid hue (par. 6): pale color
vanquished (par. 15): defeated
temerity (par. 15): nerve
teeming (par. 16): crowded

17   A neighbor, a woman, complained to the mayor, Judge Stevens, eighty years old.

18   "But what will you have me to do about it, madam?" he said.

19   "Why, send her word to stop it," the woman said. "Isn't there a law?"

20   "I'm sure that won't be necessary," Judge Stevens said. "It's probably just a snake or a rat that nigger of hers killed in the yard. I'll speak to him about it."

21   The next day he received two more complaints, one from a man who came in diffident deprecation. "We really must do something about it, Judge. I'd be the last one in the world to bother Miss Emily, but we've got to do something." That night the Board of Aldermen met—three graybeards and one younger man, a member of the rising generation.

22   "It's simple enough," he said. "Send her word to have her place cleaned up. Give her a certain time to do it in, and if she don't . . . "

23   "Dammit, sir," Judge Stevens said, "will you accuse a lady to her face of smelling bad?"

24   So the next night, after midnight, four men crossed Miss Emily's lawn and slunk about the house like burglars, sniffing along the base of the brickwork and at the cellar openings while one of them performed a regular sowing motion with his hand out of a sack slung from his shoulder. They broke open the cellar door and sprinkled lime there, and in all the outbuildings. As they recrossed the lawn, a window that had been dark was lighted and Miss Emily sat in it, the light behind her, and her upright torso motionless as that of an idol. They crept quietly across the lawn and into the shadow of the locusts that lined the street. After a week or two the smell went away.

25   That was when people had begun to feel really sorry for her. People in our town, remembering how old lady Wyatt, her great-aunt, had gone completely crazy at last, believed that the Griersons held themselves a little too high for what they really were. None of the young men were quite good enough for Miss Emily and such. We had long thought of them as a tableau, Miss Emily a slender figure in white in the background, her father a spraddled silhouette in the foreground, his back to her and clutching a horsewhip, the two of them framed by the back-flung front door. So when she got to be thirty and was still single, we were not pleased exactly, but vindicated; even with insanity in the family she wouldn't have turned down all of her chances if they had really materialized.

26   When her father died, it got about that the house was all that was left to her, and in a way, people were glad. At last they could pity Miss Emily. Being

NOTES

diffident (par. 21): hesitant

deprecation (par. 21): mild disapproval

sowing (par. 24): scattering

torso (par. 24): upper body

tableau (par. 25): like a posed picture

spraddled (par. 25): spread out

silhouette (par. 25): literally, the outline of some figure

vindicated (par. 25): proven correct

materialized (par. 25): occurred

left alone, and a pauper, she had become humanized. Now she too would know the old thrill and the old despair of a penny more or less.

27   The day after his death all the ladies prepared to call at the house and offer condolence and aid, as is our custom. Miss Emily met them at the door, dressed as usual and with no trace of grief on her face. She told them that her father was not dead. She did that for three days, with the ministers calling on her, and the doctors, trying to persuade her to let them dispose of the body. Just as they were about to resort to law and force, she broke down, and they buried her father quickly.

28   We did not say she was crazy then. We believed she had to do that. We remembered all the young men her father had driven away, and we knew that with nothing left, she would have to cling to that which had robbed her, as people will.

III

29   She was sick for a long time. When we saw her again, her hair was cut short, making her look like a girl, with a vague resemblance to those angels in colored church windows—sort of tragic and serene.

30   The town had just let the contracts for paving the sidewalks, and in the summer after her father's death they began the work. The construction company came with niggers and mules and machinery, and a foreman named Homer Barron, a Yankee—a big, dark, ready man, with a big voice and eyes lighter than his face. The little boys would follow in groups to hear him cuss the niggers, and the niggers singing in time to the rise and fall of picks. Pretty soon he knew everybody in town. Whenever you heard a lot of laughing anywhere about the square, Homer Barron would be in the center of the group. Presently, we began to see him and Miss Emily on Sunday afternoons driving in the yellow-wheeled buggy and the matched team of bays from the livery stable.

31   At first we were glad that Miss Emily would have an interest, because the ladies all said, "Of course a Grierson would not think seriously of a Northerner, a day laborer." But there were still others, older people, who said that even grief could not cause a real lady to forget *noblesse oblige*—without calling it *noblesse oblige*. They just said, "Poor Emily. Her kinsfolk should come to her." She had some kin in Alabama; but years ago her father had fallen out with them over the estate of old lady Wyatt, the crazy woman, and there was no communication between the two families. They had not even been represented at the funeral.

32   And as soon as the old people said, "Poor Emily," the whispering began. "Do you suppose it's really so?" they said to one another. "Of course it is.

NOTES

pauper (par. 26): a very poor person

condolence (par. 27): sympathy

serene (par. 29): peaceful

let (par. 30): issued

noblesse oblige (par. 31): Literally, "nobility obligates." The term refers to the obligation of a person of high standing to be honorable and generous.

What else could . . . ” This behind their hands; rustling of craned silk and satin behind jalousies closed upon the sun of Sunday afternoon as the thin, swift clop-clop-clop of the matched team passed: “Poor Emily.”

33   She carried her head high enough—even when we believed that she was fallen. It was as if she demanded more than ever the recognition of her dignity as the last Grierson; as if it had wanted that touch of earthiness to reaffirm her imperviousness. Like when she bought the rat poison, the arsenic. That was over a year after they had begun to say “Poor Emily,” and while the two female cousins were visiting her.

34   “I want some poison,” she said to the druggist. She was over thirty then, still a slight woman, though thinner than usual, with cold, haughty black eyes in a face the flesh of which was strained across the temples and about the eye-sockets as you imagine a lighthouse-keeper’s face ought to look. “I want some poison,” she said.

35   “Yes, Miss Emily. What kind? For rats and such? I’d recom—”

36   “I want the best you have. I don’t care what kind.”

37   The druggist named several. “They’ll kill anything up to an elephant. But what you want is—”

38   “Arsenic,” Miss Emily said. “Is that a good one?”

39   “Is . . . arsenic? Yes, ma’am. But what you want—”

40   “I want arsenic.”

41   The druggist looked down at her. She looked back at him, erect, her face like a strained flag. “Why, of course,” the druggist said. “If that’s what you want. But the law requires you to tell what you are going to use it for.”

42   Miss Emily just stared at him, her head tilted back in order to look him eye for eye, until he looked away and went and got the arsenic and wrapped it up. The Negro delivery boy brought her the package; the druggist didn’t come back. When she opened the package at home there was written on the box, under the skull and bones: “For rats.”

IV

43   So the next day we all said, “She will kill herself”; and we said it would be the best thing. When she had first begun to be seen with Homer Barron, we had said, “She will marry him.” Then we said, “She will persuade him yet,” because Homer himself had remarked—he liked men, and it was known that he drank with the younger men in the Elks’ Club—that he was not a marrying man. Later we said, “Poor Emily” behind the jalousies as they passed on Sunday afternoon in the glittering buggy, Miss Emily with her head high and Homer Barron with his hat cocked and a cigar in his teeth, reins and whip in a yellow glove.

44   Then some of the ladies began to say that it was a disgrace to the town and a bad example to the young people. The men did not want to interfere,

NOTES

jalousies (par. 32): blinds
reaffirm (par. 33): prove again
imperviousness (par. 33): ability to be affected by nothing

but at last the ladies forced the Baptist minister—Miss Emily's people were Episcopal—to call upon her. He would never divulge what happened during that interview, but he refused to go back again. The next Sunday they again drove about the streets, and the following day the minister's wife wrote to Miss Emily's relations in Alabama.

45   So she had blood-kin under her roof again and we sat back to watch developments. At first nothing happened. Then we were sure that they were to be married. We learned that Miss Emily had been to the jeweler's and ordered a man's toilet set in silver, with the letters H. B. on each piece. Two days later we learned that she had bought a complete outfit of men's clothing, including a nightshirt, and we said, "They are married." We were really glad. We were glad because the two female cousins were even more Grierson than Miss Emily had ever been.

46   So we were not surprised when Homer Barron—the streets had been finished some time since—was gone. We were a little disappointed that there was not a public blowing-off, but we believed that he had gone on to prepare for Miss Emily's coming, or to give her a chance to get rid of the cousins. (By that time it was a cabal, and we were all Miss Emily's allies to help circumvent the cousins.) Sure enough, after another week they departed. And, as we had expected all along, within three days Homer Barron was back in town. A neighbor saw the Negro man admit him at the kitchen door at dusk one evening.

47   And that was the last we saw of Homer Barron. And of Miss Emily for some time. The Negro man went in and out with the market basket, but the front door remained closed. Now and then we would see her at the window for a moment, as the men did that night when they sprinkled the lime, but for almost six months she did not appear on the streets. Then we knew that this was to be expected too; as if that quality of her father which had thwarted her woman's life so many times had been too virulent and too furious to die.

48   When we next saw Miss Emily, she had grown fat and her hair was turning gray. During the next few years it grew grayer and grayer until it attained an even pepper-and-salt iron-gray, when it ceased turning. Up to the day of her death at seventy-four it was still that vigorous iron-gray, like the hair of an active man.

49   From that time on her front door remained closed, save for a period of six or seven years, when she was about forty, during which she gave lessons in china-painting. She fitted up a studio in one of the downstairs rooms, where the daughters and granddaughters of Colonel Sartoris' contemporaries were sent to her with the same regularity and in the same spirit that they were sent to church on Sundays with a twenty-five-cent piece for the collection plate. Meanwhile her taxes had been remitted.

NOTES

divulge (par. 44): reveal

a man's toilet set (par. 45): personal items such as a hairbrush, a razor, and so on

cabal (par. 46): a group of people united to bring about a certain result

circumvent (par. 46): outsmart

thwarted (par. 47): frustrated

virulent (par. 47): poisonous

50   Then the newer generation became the backbone and the spirit of the town, and the painting pupils grew up and fell away and did not send their children to her with boxes of color and tedious brushes and pictures cut from the ladies' magazines. The front door closed upon the last one and remained closed for good. When the town got free postal delivery, Miss Emily alone refused to let them fasten the metal numbers above her door and attach a mailbox to it. She would not listen to them.

51   Daily, monthly, yearly we watched the Negro grow grayer and more stooped, going in and out with the market basket. Each December we sent her a tax notice, which would be returned by the post office a week later, unclaimed. Now and then we would see her in one of the downstairs windows—she had evidently shut up the top floor of the house—like the carven torso of an idol in a niche, looking or not looking at us, we could never tell which. Thus, she passed from generation to generation—dear, inescapable, impervious, tranquil, and perverse.

52   And so she died. Fell ill in the house filled with dust and shadows, with only a doddering Negro man to wait on her. We did not even know she was sick; we had long since given up trying to get any information from the Negro. He talked to no one, probably not even to her, for his voice had grown harsh and rusty, as if from disuse.

53   She died in one of the downstairs rooms, in a heavy walnut bed with a curtain, her gray head propped on a pillow yellow and moldy with age and lack of sunlight.

V

54   The Negro met the first of the ladies at the front door and let them in, with their hushed, sibilant voices and their quick, curious glances, and then he disappeared. He walked right through the house and out the back and was not seen again.

55   The two female cousins came at once. They held the funeral on the second day, with the town coming to look at Miss Emily beneath a mass of bought flowers, with the crayon face of her father musing profoundly above the bier and the ladies sibilant and macabre; and the very old men—some in their brushed Confederate uniforms—on the porch and the lawn, talking of Miss Emily as if she had been a contemporary of theirs, believing that they had danced with her and courted her perhaps, confusing time with its mathematical progression, as the old do, to whom all the past is not a diminished road but, instead, a huge meadow which no winter ever quite touches, divided from them now by the narrow bottleneck of the most recent decade of years.

NOTES

tedious (par. 50): tiresome

niche (par. 51): literally, a recess in a wall in which a statue is usually placed

tranquil (par. 51): calm

perverse (par. 51): extremely strange

sibilant (par. 54): hissing

bier (par. 55): a stand upon which a coffin is placed

macabre (par. 55): fascinated with death

a contemporary (par. 55): a person of approximately the same age

56   Already we knew that there was one room in that region above stairs which no one had seen in forty years, and which would have to be forced. They waited until Miss Emily was decently in the ground before they opened it.

57   The violence of breaking down the door seemed to fill this room with pervading dust. A thin, acrid pall as of the tomb seemed to lie everywhere upon this room decked and furnished as for a bridal: upon the valance curtains of faded rose color, upon the rose-shaded lights, upon the dressing table, upon the delicate array of crystal and the man's toilet things backed with tarnished silver, silver so tarnished that the monogram was obscured. Among them lay a collar and tie, as if they had just been removed, which lifted, left upon the surface a pale crescent in the dust. Upon a chair hung the suit, carefully folded; beneath it the two mute shoes and the discarded socks.

58   The man himself lay in the bed.

59   For a long while we just stood there, looking down at the profound and fleshless grin. The body had apparently once lain in the attitude of an embrace, but now the long sleep that outlasts love, that conquers even the grimace of love, had cuckolded him. What was left of him, rotted beneath what was left of the nightshirt, had become inextricable from the bed in which he lay; and upon him and upon the pillow beside him lay that even coating of the patient and bidding dust.

60   Then we noticed that in the second pillow was the indentation of a head. One of us lifted something from it, and leaning forward, that faint and invisible dust dry and acrid in the nostrils, we saw a long strand of iron-gray hair.

NOTES

acrid (par. 57): harsh, irritating

pall (par. 57): atmosphere of gloom

profound (par. 59): difficult to understand

grimace (par. 59): a facial expression

cuckolded (par. 59): literally, a cuckold is a man whose wife is unfaithful to him

inextricable (par. 59): inseparable

Life after High School

Joyce Carol Oates

1   "Sunny? Sun-ny?"

2   On that last night of March, 1959, in soiled sheepskin parka and unbuckled overshoes, but bareheaded in the lightly falling snow, Zachary Graff, eighteen years old, six feet one and a half inches tall, weight 203 pounds, IQ 160, stood beneath Sunny Burhman's second-story bedroom window, calling her name softly, urgently, as if his very life depended on it. It was nearly midnight: Sunny had been in bed for a half hour, and woke from a thin dissolving sleep to hear her name rising mysteriously out of the dark, the voice low, gravelly,

NOTE

parka (par. 2): coat with a hood

repetitive as the surf. "Sun-*ny*?" She had not spoken with Zachary Graff since the previous week, when she'd told him, quietly, tears shining in her eyes, that she did not love him; she could not accept his engagement ring, still less marry him. This was the first time in the twelve weeks of Zachary's pursuit of her that he'd dared to come to the rear of the Burhmans' house, by day or night—the first time, as Sunny would say afterward, that he'd ever appealed to her in such a way.

3   They would ask, In what way?

4   Sunny would hesitate, and say, So—emotionally. In a way that scared me.

5   So you sent him away?

6   She did. She sent him away.

7   It was much talked of at South Lebanon High School, how, in this winter of their senior year, Zachary Graff, who had never to anyone's recollection asked a girl out before, let alone pursued her so publicly and with such clumsy devotion, seemed to have fallen in love with Sunny Burhman.

8   Of all people—Sunny Burhman.

9   Odd, too, that Zachary should seem to have discovered Sunny only now, though the two had been classmates in the South Lebanon, New York, public schools since first grade.

10   Zachary, whose father was Homer Graff, the town's pre-eminent physician, had since ninth grade cultivated a clipped, mock-gallant manner when speaking with female classmates—his Clifton Webb style. He was unfailingly courteous, but unfailingly cool, measured, formal. He seemed impervious to the giddy rise and ebb of adolescent emotion, moving, clumsy but determined, like a grizzly bear on its hind legs, through the school corridors, rarely glancing to left or right: his gaze, its myopia corrected by lenses encased in chunky black-plastic frames, was firmly fixed on the horizon. Dr. Graff's son was not so much unpopular as feared, and thus disliked.

11   If Zachary's excellent academic record continued uninterrupted through final papers and final exams, and no one suspected that it would not, Zachary would be valedictorian of the class of 1959. Barbara ("Sunny") Burhman, later to distinguish herself at Cornell, would graduate only ninth, in a class of eighty-two.

12   Zachary's attentiveness to Sunny had begun, with no warning, immediately after Christmas recess, when classes resumed in January. Suddenly, a half-dozen times a day, in Sunny's vicinity, looming large, eyeglasses glittering, there Zachary was. His Clifton Webb pose had dissolved; he was shy, stammering, yet forceful, even bold, waiting for the advantageous moment

---

NOTES

pre-eminent (par. 10): most notable

mock-gallant (par. 10): exaggeratedly courteous

Clifton Webb (par. 10): American actor (1893–1966)

impervious to (par. 10): unaffected by

giddy (par. 10): flighty

myopia (par. 10): nearsightedness

valedictorian (par. 11): the student with the best grades

(for Sunny was always surrounded by friends) to push forward and say, "Hi, Sunny!" The greeting, utterly commonplace in content, sounded in Zachary's mouth like a Latin phrase torturously translated.

13   Sunny, so named for her really quite astonishing smile, a dazzling white Sunny-smile that transformed a girl of conventional freckled, snub-nosed prettiness into a true beauty, might have been surprised initially but gave no sign, saying "Hi, Zach!"

14   In those years the corridors of South Lebanon High School were lyric crossfires of *Hi!* and *H'lo!* and *Good to see ya!* uttered hundreds of times daily by the golden girls, the popular, confident, good-looking girls—club officers, prom queens, cheerleaders like Sunny Burhman and her friends—tossed out indiscriminately, for that was the style.

15   Most of the students were in fact practicing Christians, of Lutheran, Presbyterian, and Methodist stock. Like Sunny Burhman, who was, or seemed, even at the time of this story, too good to be true. That's to say—*good*.

16   So, though Sunny soon wondered why on earth Zachary Graff was hanging around her, why, again, at her elbow, or lying in wait for her at the foot of a stairway, why, for the nth time that week, *him*, she was too *good* to indicate impatience or exasperation—too *good* to tell him, as her friends advised, to get lost.

17   He telephoned her too. Poor Zachary. Stammering over the phone, his voice lowered as if he were in terror of being overheard, "Is S-Sunny there, Mrs. B-Burhman? May I speak with her, please?" And Mrs. Burhman, who knew Dr. Graff and his wife, of course, since everyone in South Lebanon, population 3,800, knew everyone else or knew of them, including frequently their family histories and facts about them of which their children were entirely unaware, hesitated, and said, "Yes, I'll put her on, but I hope you won't talk long—Sunny has homework tonight." Or, apologetically but firmly, "No, I'm afraid she isn't here. May I take a message?"

18   "N-no message," Zachary murmured, and hurriedly hung up.

19   Sunny, standing close by, thumbnail in the just perceptible gap between her front teeth, expression crinkled in dismay, whispered, "Oh, Mom. I feel so *bad*. I just feel so—*bad*."

20   Mrs. Burhman said briskly, "You don't have time for all of them, honey."

21   Still, Zachary was not discouraged, and in time their schoolmates began to observe Sunny engaged in conversations with him—the two of them sitting alone in a corner of the cafeteria, or walking together after a meeting of the Debate Club, of which Zachary was president and Sunny a member. They were both on the staff of the South Lebanon High *Beacon* and the 1959 South Lebanon High yearbook and the South Lebanon *Torch* (the literary magazine). They were both members of the National Honor Society and the

NOTES

conventional (par. 13): usual

lyric (par. 14): musical

indiscriminately (par. 14): unselectively

exasperation (par. 16): annoyance

dismay (par. 19): distress

Quill & Scroll Society. Though Zachary Graff, in his aloofness and impatience with most of his peers, would be remembered as antisocial—a "loner," in fact—his record of activities, printed beneath his photograph in the yearbook, suggested that he had time, or made time, for things that mattered to him.

22   He shunned sports, however. High school sports, at least. His life's game, he informed Sunny Burhman, unaware of the solemn pomposity with which he spoke, would be *golf*. His father had been instructing him informally since his twelfth birthday.

23   Zachary said, "I have no natural talent for it, and I find it profoundly boring, but golf will be my game." And he pushed his chunky black glasses roughly against the bridge of his nose, something he did countless times a day, as if they were in danger of sliding off.

24   Zachary Graff had such a physical presence that few of his contemporaries would have described him as unattractive, still less as homely. His head appeared oversized, even for his massive body; his eyes were deep-set, with a look of watchfulness and secrecy; his skin was tallow-colored and blemished in wavering patches like topographical maps. His big teeth glinted with filaments of silver, and his breath, oddly for one whose father was a doctor, was stale, musty—not that Sunny Burhman ever mentioned this fact to others.

25   Her friends began to ask, a bit jealously, reproachfully, "What do you two talk about so much—you and *him*?" and Sunny replied, taking care not to hint with the slightest movement of her eyebrows, or rolling of her eyes, that, yes, she found the situation peculiar too, "Oh—Zachary and I talk about all kinds of things. *He* talks, mainly. He's brilliant. He's" —pausing, her forehead delicately crinkling in thought, her lovely brown eyes for a moment clouded— "well, *brilliant*."

26   In fact, at first Zachary spoke, in his intense, obsessive way, of impersonal subjects: the meaning of life, the future of Earth, whether science or art best satisfies the human hunger for self-expression. He said, laughing nervously, fixing Sunny with his bold stare, "Just to pose certain questions is, I guess, to show your hope that they can be answered."

27   Early on, Zachary seemed to have understood that if he expressed doubt about "whether God exists," and so forth, Sunny Burhman would listen seriously, and would talk with him earnestly, with the air of a nurse giving a transfusion to a patient in danger of expiring from loss of blood. She was not a

NOTES

aloofness (par. 21): indifference toward

antisocial (par. 21): not sociable

shunned (par. 22): purposely avoided

pomposity (par. 22): self-importance

contemporaries (par. 24): peers

tallow (par. 24): hard animal fat used to make candles and soap

topographical maps (par. 24): maps that show the surface features (such as elevation) of a place or region

filaments (par. 24): threads

reproachfully (par. 25): disapprovingly

giving a transfusion (par. 27): putting blood into the bloodstream

expiring (par. 27): dying

religious fanatic but she *was* a devout Christian; the Burhmans were members of the First Presbyterian Church of South Lebanon, and Sunny was president of her youth group and, among other good deeds, did YWCA volunteer work on Saturday afternoons; she had not the slightest doubt that Jesus Christ— that is to say, His spirit—dwelled in her heart, and that simply by speaking the truth of what she believed, she could convince others.

28   Though one day soon Sunny would examine her beliefs, and question the faith into which she'd been born, she had not yet done so. She was a virgin, and virginal in all, or most, of her thoughts.

29   Sometimes, behind her back, even by friends, Sunny was laughed at, gently—never ridiculed, for no one would ridicule Sunny.

30   When popular Chuck Crueller, a quarterback for the South Lebanon varsity football team, was injured during a game and carried off by ambulance to undergo emergency surgery, Sunny mobilized the other cheerleaders, tears fierce in her eyes: "We can do it for Chuck—we can *pray*." And so the eight girls in their short-skirted crimson jumpers and starched white cotton blouses had gripped one another's hands tightly, and weeping, on the verge of hysteria, had prayed, prayed, *prayed*—hidden away in the depths of the girls' locker room for hours. Sunny had led the prayers, and Chuck Crueller had recovered.

31   So you wouldn't ridicule Sunny Burhman. Somehow it wouldn't be appropriate.

32   As her classmate Tobias Shanks wrote of her, in his function as literary editor of the 1959 South Lebanon literary yearbook: "*Sunny Burhman!—an all-American girl too good to be true who is nonetheless TRUE!*"

33   If Tobias Shanks's praise obscured a slyly mocking tone, a hint that such goodness was predictable and superficial, perhaps of no genuine merit, the caption, mere print, beneath Sunny's dazzlingly beautiful photograph conveyed nothing but admiration and affection.

34   Surprisingly, for all his pose of skepticism and superiority, Zachary Graff, too, was a Christian. He'd been baptized Lutheran, and never failed to attend Sunday services with his parents at the First Lutheran Church. Amid the congregation of somber, somnambulant worshippers, Zachary Graff's frowning young face, the set of his beefy shoulders, drew the minister's uneasy eye; some parishioners murmured of Dr. Graff's precocious son, in retrospect, that he'd been perhaps too *serious*.

NOTES

fanatic (par. 27): extremist
devout (par. 27): faithful, sincere
mobilized (par. 30): assembled and motivated
hysteria (par. 30): an uncontrollable outburst of emotion
obscured (par. 33): concealed
slyly mocking (par. 33): secretly scornful
superficial (par. 33): shallow
merit (par. 33): worth
skepticism (par. 34): doubt
somnambulant (par. 34): sleepwalking
precocious (par. 34): gifted
in retrospect (par. 34): looking back (in time)

35   Before falling in love with Sunny Burhman, and discussing his religious doubts with her, Zachary had often discussed them with Tobias Shanks, who'd been his friend, you might say his only friend, since seventh grade. (But only sporadically since seventh grade, because the boys, each highly intelligent and inclined to impatience and sarcasm, got on each other's nerves.) Once, Zachary confided in Tobias that he prayed every morning of his life. Immediately upon waking he scrambled out of bed, knelt, hid his face in his hands, and prayed—for his sinful soul, for his sinful thoughts, deeds, desires. He lacerated his soul the way he'd been taught by his mother to tug a fine-toothed steel comb through his coarse, oily hair: never less than once a day.

36   Tobias Shanks, a self-proclaimed agnostic since the age of fourteen, laughed and asked derisively, "Yes, but what do you pray *for*, exactly?" Zachary had thought a bit and said, not ironically, but altogether seriously, "To get through the day. Doesn't everyone?"

37   Zachary's parents urged him to go to Muhlenberg College, which was church-affiliated; Zachary hoped to go elsewhere. He said humbly to Sunny Burhman, "If you go to Cornell, Sunny, I—maybe I'll go there too?"

38   Sunny hesitated and then smiled. "Oh. That would be nice."

39   "You wouldn't mind, Sunny?"

40   "Why would I *mind*, Zachary?" Sunny laughed, to hide her impatience. They were headed for Zachary's car, parked just up the hill from the YM-YWCA building. It was a gusty Saturday afternoon in early March. Leaving the YWCA, Sunny had seen Zachary Graff standing at the curb as if accidentally, his hands in the pockets of his sheepskin parka, his head lowered but his eyes nervously alert.

41   She couldn't avoid him, and so had to allow him to drive her home. She was beginning to feel panic, however, like darting tongues of flame, at the prospect of Zachary Graff always *there*.

42   Tell the creep to get lost, her friends counseled. Even her nice friends were unsentimental about Zachary Graff.

43   Until sixth grade Sunny had been plain little Barbara Burhman. Then, one day, her teacher had said to all the class, in one of those moments of inspiration that can alter, by whim, the course of an entire life, "Tell you what, boys and girls: let's call Barbara 'Sunny' from now on—that's what she *is*."

44   Ever afterward in South Lebanon she was "Sunny" Burhman. Plain little Barbara had been left behind, seemingly forever.

45   So of course Sunny could not tell Zachary Graff to get lost. Such words were not part of her vocabulary.

NOTES

sporadically (par. 35): irregularly

lacerated (par. 35): distressed

agnostic (par. 36): one who neither believes nor disbelieves in the existence of God, maintaining that one cannot know whether or not God exists

derisively (par. 36): scornfully

prospect (par. 41): possibility

whim (par. 43): a sudden impulse

one of the two most popular Web sites for students across grades 4–12. (The other site is YouTube.) We would like to summarize our shared concerns and address the issues that impact our students, and our communities.

2   Note: Though this article targets Facebook specifically because of its popularity, the article also applies to the many other social networks our students frequent. They include YouTube, MySpace, Hi5, Friendster, Xanga, DeviantArt, and others.

3   **1. For Those Schools That Allow It, the Use of Facebook in Our Communities Can Take an Inordinate Amount of Internet Bandwidth.**

4   And for those schools that allow access to Facebook, how do we reconcile our concerns that younger and younger children are using this adult social network? Four years ago it was rare to learn of a child under 7th grade with an account. Last fall, for the first time, 4th graders began reporting to us that they had Facebook accounts. We now estimate that about 60–70% of 7th graders have accounts and the number is higher for 8th graders. These children are too young to be using Facebook or other adult social networks for the reasons detailed below.

5   **2. Using Facebook Takes Time. Often, a Lot of Time!**

6   The greatest motivating factor for children to use technology in grades 7 and up is to connect to others; to socialize. Their irresistible need to connect with their peers, coupled with the development of 24/7 accessible technologies, can make the use of sites like Facebook all-consuming. We have concerns for children and teens today growing up in a world where they are wired 24/7 without a break. For many of our kids there is little or no "down time." Some have difficulty disengaging from their social life. For some, it even raises their anxiety level to be without their cell phones for a few hours! We do not believe this is healthy for them.

7   **3. To Students Using Facebook, There Is a False Sense of Privacy.**

8   Couple this false sense of privacy with the feeling of anonymity and lack of social responsibility that often develops from using text-centered telecommunications, and we see that many students post embarrassing, humiliating, denigrating, and hurtful content in both text, photos, and videos. We need to teach them that NOTHING IS PRIVATE online, especially their social

NOTES

The use of Facebook . . . can take an inordinate amount of Internet bandwidth. (par. 3): The use of Facebook . . . can slow down the speed at which data is transmitted to and from computers over the Internet.

reconcile (par. 4): find a solution to

irresistible (par. 6): overwhelming

peers (par. 6): classmates

accessible (par. 6): easy to use

denigrating (par. 8): disrespecting

networks. We need to show them examples of the serious consequences that have occurred to those whose egregious online behavior has been made public. Students have been expelled from high schools and colleges. Students have been denied acceptances to intern programs, admission to independent high schools, colleges, and jobs at summer camps. Students and their families have been sued for slander and defamation of character. Students and their parents have been arrested. All because of the content they have posted in their "private" social network accounts. People are trolling their accounts. Hackers, scammers, reporters, police, high school and college admissions officers, employers, parents, and summer camp directors. . . . Adults ARE looking and the kids do not get it! Also, they do not realize the instant they post something to Facebook (or MySpace or YouTube, etc.), they have just lost control and ownership of that content. Try reviewing the privacy rights of Facebook with your middle and high school students. It is quite an eye opener!

9   In fall 2007, Dr. Nora Barnes, Director for the Center of Marketing Research at University of Massachusetts Dartmouth, published a study that showed more than 20% of colleges and universities search social networks for their admissions candidates. Do you think that percentage will decrease, increase, or remain unchanged in the coming years? Ask your high school students that question!

10   Students often ask us, "How can anyone possibly get into my private Facebook pages?" Here are the most common methods and a link to a sample article about each:

11   a) Security and software flaws are exposed. Software is hacked.

> —Tech & Learning Advisor Blog. "My Facebook account was hacked!" by Cheryl Oakes (http://www.techlearning.com/blogs.aspx?id=15098).

12   b) Accounts are phished when users are tricked into clicking an email or IM link taking them to fake login pages. Once phished, scammers use various applications to suck out personal information from a user's entire network of friends. Scammers try using the phished information, including the login

---

NOTES

egregious (par. 8): awful

intern programs (par. 8): training programs

slander (par. 5): untrue verbal statements that harm another person's reputation

defamation of character (par. 8): false statements (verbal or written) that harm another person's reputation

trolling (par. 8): secretly searching

hackers (par. 8): persons who can get around computer security measures

scammers (par. 8): persons who commit fraud

privacy rights (par. 8): Web sites vary in the degree to which they protect their users' privacy or personal information (names, addresses, income, interests, etc.). Some sites disclose no information. Others provide some or all of their users' information to other sites, businesses, marketing agencies, and so forth. Typically, users have to agree to a Web sites privacy policies before they can use the site. Many (if not most) agree to those policies without ever reading them.

phished (par. 12): Phishing is the attempt to trick people into providing sensitive information (user names, passwords, credit card numbers, etc.) in order to steal from them.

password, to access banks and credit card accounts because they know that most people have one password for all their accounts. They also target teens' Facebook accounts because they have learned that a small percent of their parents use combinations of their children's names and birthdays as passwords to their financial and credit card accounts.

> —Tech Crunch. "Phishing scam targeting Facebook users" by Duncan Riley (http://www.techcrunch.com/2008/03/26/phishing-scam-targeting-facebook-users/).

> —*Wired.* "Fraudsters target Facebook with phishing scam" by Ryan Singel (http://www.wired.com/politics/security/news/2008/01/facebook_phish).

> —The Next Web. "Facebook under massive phishing attack from China" by Steven Carrol (http://thenextweb.com/2008/08/10/facebook-under-massive-phishing-attack-from-china/).

13   c) Perhaps the most common reason that teens' private information is exposed is because they are easily tricked into accepting friend requests from strangers. Though there is not a lot of research available on this point, some research and informal studies suggest that teens allow into their Facebook networks 44%–87% of the strangers that knock on their door. This trick is best described as the "wolf in sheep's clothing." Many kids, especially girls, have a difficult time saying "no" to a "friend" request.

> —C-net News. "Facebook users pretty willing to add strangers as 'friends'" by Caroline McCarthy (http://news.cnet.com/8301-10784_3-9759401-7.html).

14   d) Students' passwords are easily guessed or hacked with readily available "cracking" software. We've met 5th graders who have demonstrated knowledge of using hacking tools such as password crackers. There are numerous examples of kids' accounts being hacked simply because someone guessed or figured out their password. Last September Gov. Sarah Palin's personal e-mail account was broken into when the hacker figured out that her password was a combination of her zip code and birth date.

> —CNN Politics.com. "Agents search apartment in Palin e-mail investigation" from Terry Frieden (http://www.cnn.com/2008/POLITICS/09/22/palin.email.probe/index.html).

15   Note: Police, and other investigative authorities such as the FBI, can have access to "private" Facebook pages. Also, we strongly suspect that Facebook itself sells access to information posted on private pages to third party marketers willing to pay the fees. At least, that was what one former employee in the social network industry who wished to remain anonymous described to us.

NOTES

wolf in sheep's clothing (par. 13): an enemy disguised as a friend
cracking (par. 14): security code breaking
third party marketers (par. 15): other businesses

16 **4. There Are Thousands of Scams Targeting Teens in Their Social Networks, Especially Facebook and MySpace.**

17   These communities are predicated on a certain level of trust. Our students, though very knowledgeable about using technology, are often naive and easily manipulated (though they would hate to think so). A simple example is a scam that hit Facebook users late last fall. Many teens had their accounts phished and the phishers sent out posts from those accounts to their friends that said "OMG! There are some photos of you on this Web site," along with a link to the Web site. The Web site showed hazy photos in the background that were hard to make out and appeared to be somewhat pornographic. A popup told the visitor they would have to register for an account in order to view photos on the site. We're certain that many kids were tricked into revealing a lot of personal information in this scam. In another scam that targeted MySpace in the last couple of years, more than 14,000 users were tricked by fake MySpace pages into visiting music Web sites to purchase music for $2–3 per album. Instead of getting music, the site charged their credit cards $300–600. Kids are easily fooled. They want to believe what is said to them, especially when it appears that others believe. Scammers use this trick against them by creating thousands of fake pages on social networks that talk about bogus Web sites to buy stuff, products that do not work (e.g., herbal medicines) and cool pages that only result in drive-by spyware downloads.

18 **5. Spyware and Adware Installations Are Very Serious Concerns.**

19   Those of us with PCs running Windows OS in our schools already devote a great deal of time, money, and other resources to these threats. Giving kids access to social networks in our school environments greatly exacerbates these threats. We need to teach our students that "Free" usually has a price when it comes to the Internet. We need to teach them how to try to determine if software, such as a Facebook add-on, is likely a disguised piece of malware. (Much of it is!)

> —PC Advisor. "Warning over malicious Facebook wall videos: Hackers target users with fake Flash download" by Juan Carlos Perez (http://www.pcadvisor.co.uk/news/index.cfm?newsid=102800).
>
> —Sophos. "Facebook users struck by new 'court jester' malware attack posts on your Facebook wall may lead to Trojan horse infection" (http://sophos.com/pressoffice/news/articles/2008/08/facebook.html).
>
> —The Register. "Link spammers go on social networking rampage" by John Leyden (http://www.theregister.co.uk/2008/04/02/facebook_spam/).

NOTES

predicated (par. 17): built

naive (par. 17): trusting

manipulated (par. 17): influenced

scam (par. 17): fraud

bogus (par. 17): fake

spyware (par. 17): software that is secretly placed on a computer to collect information about the user and relay it to the programmer

OS (par. 19): Operating system. An operating system manages the other software programs on a computer.

exacerbates (par. 19): worsens

malware (par. 19): software that is intended to harm a computer

20   Note: "Mac owners" are not completely off the hook. Last June, the first three spyware apps were discovered against the Mac OS and late last fall there was evidence of hijack-ware successfully targeting Firefox on a Mac. In April, 2009, the first Mac Botnet, in which scammers take control of Apple Mac computers to send out spam, was reported.

21   ## 6. We Need to Acknowledge That Screens Act as a Moral Disconnect for Many of Our Students.

22   Every day online there are thousands of kids who say mean and hurtful things because they can. They are increasingly living their social lives in a world without caring, loving adults watching out for them, without expectations for their behavior, and without boundaries. Research shows that children grow up healthiest in a world with love, communication, structure, and boundaries. These qualities hardly exist online for our children/teens. Instead, harassing language is normalized, the sexualization of girls/women is commonplace, and the lack of supervision creates an "anything goes" wild-wild-west. Here is a simple case in point. Would Texas Longhorn lineman Buck Burnette have said the same thing about President Obama if handed a microphone at a school assembly in front of hundreds of students? Would he have written his posted statement on a large poster and held it up in downtown Houston for a few hours? We doubt it.

> —Fanhouse. "Texas' Buck Burnette learns why racist Obama Facebook updates are dumb" by Will Brinson (http://ncaafootball.fanhouse.com/2008/11/06/texas-c-buck-burnette- learns-why-racist-obama-facebook-updates-a/).

23   Students need to learn to be nice and kind to others online. They need to be respectful and thoughtful about what they say and how they act online, just as in real life. We need to do a better job of teaching them that disengaging from social responsibility while using telecommunications is not acceptable behavior.

NOTES

hijack-ware (par. 20): software that secretly redirects a computer's Web browser from a real Web site to a fake Web site

Mac Botnet (par. 20): small software programs that are secretly placed on Macintosh computers in order to collect users' personal information without their knowledge

as a moral disconnect (par. 21): without concern for how one's acts or words affect others

Buck Burnette (par. 22): University of Texas football player dismissed from the team after making a racist joke about Barack Obama in 2008

disengaging from social responsibility (par. 23): feeling no responsibility for one's behavior toward others

using telecommunications (par. 23): sending and receiving messages online

24   **7. Students Have Very Little Knowledge About How Much They Are Being Marketed To; How Their Purchasing Decisions and Attitudes Are Being Manipulated; How Their Personal Information Is Used; and Even How Valuable That Personal Information Is.**

25   Most do not understand the damage that can come from identity theft and impersonation. They are heavily targeted on Facebook and their data is heavily "scrubbed" and used. Facebook's announcement about Beacon in November 2007 brought such a huge negative assault from users that Mark Zuckerberg had to back-step and tell users that they were automatically opted OUT, rather than IN, as planned. Most users saw Beacon as a privacy nightmare. We need to help our students become more media savvy, to understand the value of personal information, and how to protect it.

> —Gigaom. "Is Facebook Beacon a privacy nightmare?" by Om Malik (http://gigaom.com/2007/11/06/facebook-beacon-privacy-issues/).

> —C-Net News. "Facebook's Zuckerberg apologizes, allows users to turn off Beacon" by Amy Tiemann (http://news.cnet.com/8301-13507_3-9829401-18.html).

> —PCMag.com. "Facebook's Zuckerberg apologizes for ads debacle" by Chloe Albanesius (http://www.pcmag.com/article2/0,2817,2228622,00.asp).

26   **8. Our Research Shows That Children and Teens Are Increasingly Using Telecommunications Technologies, Including Facebook, to Avoid Difficult Face-to-Face Conversations.**

27   For example, it saddens us to hear 16-year-olds say they would rather break up with their girlfriend/boyfriend by texting, IMing, or posting on their Facebook wall than tell them in person (or over the phone). When asked why, they'll tell you "because it's easier." We believe this avoidance will have increasingly negative ramifications on their communication skills throughout life.

28   **9. More And More, Children Are Turning to Making Friendships and Building Relationships Online.**

29   This includes the use of Facebook. Socialization skills in children are best learned in real life. Children are far too inexperienced to use telecommunications tools to make friends and build relationships in a healthy and safe manner online.

NOTES

identity theft and impersonation (par. 25): stealing someone's personal information (social security number, bank account number, credit card number, etc.) and then pretending to be that person in order to steal his or her money, open credit cards in his or her name, and so forth.
data is heavily "scrubbed" (par. 25): data is analyzed and cleansed of errors
Beacon (par. 25): a Facebook program that collected and published data about its users' activities on other Web sites. It was shut down in September 2008 because of privacy concerns.
Mark Zuckerberg (par. 25): co-founder of Facebook
media savvy (par. 25): well-informed about online communications
ramifications (par. 27): results
socialization (par. 29): acceptable behavior

30 **10. The Meaning of the Word "Friend" Is Changing for Our Students and This Change Puts Them at Risk in Several Ways.**

31   Ask an average teenager how many friends they have in their Facebook account and from some you may hear numbers between 200 and 500. "Friending" is a verb and for many of our students, some of their friends are complete strangers. We need to challenge them to think about what a friend is and consider the ways we typically value friends. Words like *trust, love, support*, and *sharing* come to mind. However, students' risks rise when they apply traditional real-life values to the "friendships" some of them develop online in sites such as Facebook.

32   We have Facebook accounts and actually see it as a wonderful and valuable resource. However, just because Facebook says that anyone 14 years or older CAN use Facebook, doesn't mean that they should. It isn't an age-appropriate or developmentally healthy place for our children and younger teens to hang out. Facebook is not working to protect our children and the laws in our country are terribly inadequate to safeguard our children online, in general. Not enough is being done to protect and educate children and teens against the risks that come from using the Internet and Facebook in particular. We (adults, parents, educators) need to do more.

33   In addition, during the last few years our schools have been welcoming an influx of a new generation of teachers. These younger teachers are typically more comfortable with technology because they have grown up with it. This presents some challenges as well. For instance, must independent schools consider setting policies for teachers regarding the use of social networks like Facebook? Should we set guidelines for the possible social interaction of our teachers with their students in sites such as Facebook? Many independent schools are currently debating these questions. Articles related to this topic make very plausible arguments for setting guidelines for teachers, as well as students.

     —SouthFloridaSun-Sentinel. "Area teachers post questionable content on Facebook" by Stephanie Horvath (http://www.sunsentinel.com/news/education/sfl-flpfacebook0601pnjun 01,0,370501.story).

34   To read other articles such as this one, visit Google and enter the words *teacher, Facebook*, and *content*. ChildrenOnline.org produces a free monthly newsletter that is designed to keep educators and parents informed about the latest issues affecting children online and to address specific questions often raised by parents and teachers.

35   One final note: The Internet is constantly changing, as are the ways that kids are using it. From recent visits to some independent schools, we have learned of a rising interest about which we are very concerned. Some middle and high school students have begun to discover online live broadcast TV, known as "social broadcasting." BlogTV.com is one such site where a visitor is able to use a built-in video camera to broadcast him or herself live on the

NOTES

an influx (par. 33): a coming in

plausible (par. 33): good

social broadcasting (par. 35): live online television or radio broadcasts

Internet. Anyone can stop by, enter a chat window, and anonymously interact with the person broadcasting. As you can imagine, without any controls, standards, or boundaries, this technology can have some serious negative consequences for some children and teens. For some of our students, using this technology can be irresistible, especially younger children who see themselves as being on real TV.

Teen "Sexting": Stupid and Illegal
Larry Magid

1   "Sexting" is the practice of taking a sexually revealing picture of yourself, typically from a cell phone, and sending it to someone. Legal consequences aside, it's a dumb thing to do, especially for younger age groups in which it has become something of a fad.

2   Even if you are comfortable with the person receiving the image, you never know for sure where else it might land. Digital images are easy to copy and forward, and even if you trust your friend's discretion, it can be accidentally forwarded or seen by others with access to your friend's phone or computer. It's not uncommon for such images to find their way to other people's cell phones and even Web pages, where they can be seen by anyone, copied, searched for, and redistributed, perhaps forever.

3   For minors, there's another risk: serious legal consequences. Creating, transmitting, and even possessing a nude, seminude, or sexually explicit image of a minor can be considered child pornography. It can be prosecuted as a state or federal felony and can even lead to having to register as a sex offender.

4   Crazy as it seems, some prosecutors have gone after kids for taking and sending pictures of themselves. There was a case in Florida a couple of years ago in which a teenage boy and girl photographed themselves nude and engaged in "unspecified sexual behavior."

5   One kid sent the picture to the other, and somehow, the police got involved. They were tried and convicted for production and distribution of child porn, and the teen who received the image had the additional charge of possession. An appeals court upheld the convictions.

6   In January this year, three teenage girls from Pennsylvania were charged for creating child porn, and the three boys who received the images were charged for possessing it. And, according to CBS News, a Texas eighth-grader in October spent a night in jail after a coach found a nude picture on his cell phone, sent by another student.

7   It's sadly ironic that the very child porn laws that were written to protect children from being exploited by adults could wind up having a devastating

NOTES

register as a sex offender (par. 3): A person convicted of a sex crime must inform police of where he or she lives and may be subject to restrictions. In some places, the information the person gives to the police is made available to the public.
exploited (par. 7): abused

impact on the lives of children who, while acting stupid, have no criminal intent. For some perspective on whether this issue is overblown, see Anne Collier's post in NetFamily News.

8   It's hard to know how prevalent the practice is. But if you believe the results of an online survey commissioned by the National Campaign to Prevent Teen and Unplanned Pregnancy, about 22 percent of teenage girls and 18 percent of boys admit to having "electronically sent, or posted online, nude or seminude pictures or video of themselves."

9   I'm not completely confident about the results of this study, which was carried out by a market research firm and not subject to academic peer review. But I think that it's fair to assume that a significant number of kids are doing this.

10   Perhaps more interesting than the survey's overall number is the breakdown of why teens take and send these pictures. Of those who reportedly sent such pictures, 71 percent of girls and 67 percent of boys said they sent or posted content to a boyfriend or girlfriend, while 21 percent of the girls and 39 percent of the boys say they sent it to someone they wanted to date.

11   As you might expect, peer pressure plays a role. Of those who sent such content, 51 percent of teen girls cited "pressure from a guy," while 18 percent of teen boys blamed pressure from girls.

12   While sexting is troubling, I think it's important for us all to take a deep breath and refrain from passing new laws or using child pornography laws that were designed to protect children from exploitation by adults.

13   I suspect that sexting will diminish over time. Kids aren't stupid and, faced with the facts, most will wise up. We also know that kids who get in trouble online are the same kids who get in trouble offline, so when teens repeatedly do sexting, or other stupid or risky things online, it's important to intervene early and often.

14   The best thing for a parent to do is to have a nonconfrontational conversation—perhaps over dinner—to ask your kids if they've heard about sexting and what they think about it.

15   You might not get a straight answer, but you'll open up a dialogue that can go a long way toward helping your kids understand how to minimize legal, social, and reputation risks. There are more tips on ConnectSafely.org, a nonprofit Internet safety site I help operate.

16   Boy, am I glad the Internet and camera phones weren't around when I was a kid.

NOTES

Anne Collier's post in NetFamily News (par. 7): http://www.netfamilynews.org/2009/03/sexting-overblown-yes-and-no.html

prevalent (par. 8): common

market research firm (par. 9): a business that researches and gathers information about customers or users of a product or service

academic peer review (par. 9): evaluation by persons qualified to judge the accuracy of the study

Steroids, Sports and the Ethics of Winning

Michael Dillingham

1   Why, ethically, does the use of steroids in sports bother us? The medical issues are fairly straightforward. The use of anabolic steroids increases the athlete's chance of getting liver cancer. Heavy or prolonged use can cause psychological and emotional problems—so-called "steroid rage."

2   Men will have testicular atrophy and libido problems, and women will have abnormal periods and changes in their normal hormonal balance.

3   Because steroids enable heavy lifting, tendon tears and osteoarthritis are common ailments. I could tell you about guys who do what their bodies weren't designed to do—such as benching 400 pounds—and by the time they are 35, they cannot lift their arms.

4   So, why do people use them? The answer to that question is also straightforward. They make you bigger, faster, and stronger. And they work perfectly well in anybody who's training heavily.

5   Should athletes be allowed to make this trade-off? Many say, "It hurts only me, so why does society care?"

6   Society cares because steroid use is a form of cheating. Since steroids work so well, they create an unfair advantage for those who take them, and this breaks the social contract athletes have implicitly agreed to: We are going to have a fair contest. There are things we can and cannot do. Even if there were a safe performance-enhancing substance, if it weren't available to everybody, using it would still be cheating.

7   Unfortunately, steroids are still ubiquitous, and one of the problems is that we let people use them. Society loves sports and tends to look the other way when they become dangerous. We tolerate boxing, where you have two guys beating each other's brains out; we tolerate sports that have severe lifetime side effects like some elements of track and field.

8   The conspirators in this are everywhere—coaches, institutions, even some parents. We see parents who are in complete denial when their kids—college

NOTES

ethics (title): morality

Michael Dillingham (author): team physician for the San Francisco 49ers and Santa Clara University

anabolic steroids (par. 1): drugs that increase muscle size

steroid rage (par. 1): angry, aggressive behavior by someone who takes large doses of steroids

testicular atrophy (par. 2): medical condition in which male reproductive organs (testes) decrease in size and may lose the ability to function

libido (par. 2): sexual desire

osteoarthritis (par. 3): a type of arthritis caused by the breakdown and loss of the cartilage between the bones of the body's joints

benching (par. 3): in other words, bench pressing (lying on bench and lifting weights into the air to increase upper body strength)

social contract (par. 6): generally agreed upon rules

implicitly (par. 6): silently and completely

ubiquitous (par. 7): everywhere

conspirators of this (par. 8): secret supporters of dangerous behavior for competitive advantage

are in complete denial (par. 8): refuse to accept unpleasant facts

athletes with eating disorders—have stress fractures of their tibias or patellas because their bones are fragile from anorexia. The parents are living through the children's achievements, so it's very difficult to break this pattern.

9   Steroid use is part of this whole youthful delusion that says, "If I just do this for a period of my life, I'll be fine. I'll smoke until I'm older; I'll only binge drink in college; I'll be anorexic or bulimic so I can run, and then I'll stop being that way and I'll go on and have a wonderful life."

10   That's playing Russian roulette, which is not a game I think we want to encourage.

11   The only things that work to discourage doping are testing and penalties. You can talk about personal responsibility until you're blue in the face, but to stop steroid use, testing is necessary. Cocaine and steroids have ceased to be big problems in professional football because of testing.

12   In most other professional sports, the inmates are running the asylum. There is no effective testing, and the penalties are pitiful. If Congress pushes this issue, and if professional sports and unions stop obstructing, and if some of the professionals get busted, we may get somewhere. I'm hopeful.

NOTES

tibia (par. 8): the larger of the two bones in the leg below the knee

patella (par. 8): knee cap

delusion (par. 9): mistaken idea

anorexic (par. 9): An anorexic refuses to eat in order to be thin.

bulimic (par. 9): A bulimic overeats and then vomits or takes laxatives to purge the digestive tract in order to be thin.

Russian roulette (par. 10): a game of chance in which participants put a single bullet in a handgun, spin the cylinder, put the muzzle against their head, and pull the trigger

inmates are running the asylum (par. 12): Literally, an *asylum* is a hospital for the mentally ill, and *inmates* are the hospital's patients.

obstructing (par. 12): interfering

Just Say Yes to Steroids—Learn, Make Better Choices

Kate Schmidt

1   The media and the public have savaged American athletes for using steroids. The case of track and field icon Marion Jones is the most recent. Last week, she tearfully returned her three gold and two bronze medals to the Olympic Committee after admitting she used steroids.

NOTES

Kate Schmidt (author): Schmidt, a participant in the 1972, 1976, and 1980 Olympics, won bronze medals in the javelin throw in '72 and '76

steroids (par. 1): drugs that increase muscle size

icon (par. 1): superstar

Marion Jones (par. 1): former world champion track and field athlete (b. 1975) who won five medals in the 2000 Olympics. She returned her medals after she admitting that she had taken steroids.

2   Much of the criticism of Jones and others caught using steroids is unfair. There is a disconnect between what the sports-viewing public knows and expects and what is actually going on. Fans have created such high expectations for athletes that success seems to require steroid use for any sport requiring speed, power or a combination of the two. The genie is out of the bottle—for good.

3   This was not always the case. When I was competing, some athletes used performance-enhancing drugs, but most didn't. I never did and still established American and world records in the javelin throw. Yet my world record was surpassed by an East German who participated in a program famous for pharmacological enhancements.

4   It is extremely difficult for an athlete to resist doing whatever it takes to win. Our culture has elevated elite athletes to a status that is good for neither them nor us. It is unhealthy and unreal.

5   Elite athletes are normal in every way except for being born with a singular skill with which they become obsessed, chasing its allure until age and injury stop them. Their natural obsession is exacerbated by $20-million signing bonuses, gold-medal tallies and fan and media insistence that elite athletes are special in every other way. Athletes are not gods. We must take them off the pedestal.

6   Fans, the media and sports governing bodies believe that we can rid sports of steroid use. Athletes always will be a step ahead of the testing labs in concealing substances because of the multibillion-dollar industries that have been built on their sweat and their obsession. They will seek out the next "thing"— a vitamin, a nutritional supplement, a training technique, a piece of training equipment, a new shoe, a drug. Athletes have used performance enhancements and supplements for centuries. We cannot change the nature of the beast.

7   Do we really think it's in the best interests of the National Football League, Major League Baseball or USA Track and Field to punish athletes—their cash cows—who test positive for steroids?

8   But follow the logic of those who would cleanse sports of drugs. In most sports, it is my belief that performance-enhancing drug use is the rule, not the exception. What would be the effects of reversing this trend? For instance, take synthetic testosterone and its derivatives out of baseball and football. What would happen?

9   There would be far fewer home runs; smaller, slower, less muscular athletes and no new records for the next few decades until human development

NOTES

The genie is out of the bottle (par. 2): In other words, once has something started, it is difficult to stop.

javelin throw (par. 3): a track and field event. A javelin is a light spear about 8 ft. long.

pharmacological (par. 3): drug

elite (par. 4): the best

allure (par. 5): attraction

exacerbated (par. 5): magnified

take them off the pedestal (par. 5): stop admiring them

cash cows (par. 7): moneymakers

synthetic (par. 8) artificial

testosterone (par. 8): a male hormone

derivatives (par. 8): drugs produced from other drugs

to two weeks, with some insurers imposing a $10,000 lifetime cap, enough to cover about ten inpatient days, or, as in Jayme's case, a $30,000 lifetime limit. All this despite studies indicating that most patients released underweight need rehospitalization. Doctors now tell seventy-pound patients they must be sicker before they can be helped, the equivalent of "sending patients with strep throat away, saying they can't be treated until it causes kidney failure," says Dr. Walter Kaye, head of the University of Pittsburgh's eating disorders program. Adds Stanford's Dr. Regina Casper: "We actually convert people into chronic patients."

5   Some doctors spend more than ten hours a week arguing with insurers. "They wear you down with untrained reviewers, then make you go through three or four levels of appeals," says Dr. Arnold Andersen, who runs an eating disorders clinic at the University of Iowa. "It's like trying to stop the ocean." Insurers generally won't reveal their rejection criteria, never see patients and make all judgments by phone. As a result, Andersen says, "every third case that needs hospitalization is not allowed in now." Dr. Elke Eckert, head of the University of Minnesota program, says that 40 percent of her patients are discharged before they should be. Adds Dr. Dean Krahn, who headed programs at the University of Michigan and the University of Wisconsin that folded because of insurance problems: "Patients gain five pounds and are discharged now. You get their anxiety up as high as it can be because they've gained weight, but you haven't had time to do anything that will help them accept it. It's torture rather than treatment." The prediction of many doctors: The 15 percent death rate will rise.

6   In recent months the problem has become even more urgent, as doctors have realized there are only a few top-notch programs left. If you have a severe eating disorder now, you may find not only that insurance won't pay for your care, you may find, as Jayme Porter did, that you have nowhere to go.

7   Back home in Stillwater, the day after she discovered the Wichita program might close, Jayme eats an apple for breakfast instead of the juice, yogurt, meat, cereal, milk, and two fruits prescribed. She heads for Oklahoma State University for the lab tests that should have been done months ago. Then she sets out on her daily walk wearing a twenty-pound knapsack that "helps me work out."

8   No one who spends a day with Jayme can wonder for long why severe anorexics need supervision. After her walk she returns to her trailer—the one her parents started out in and is now hers—parked outside the campus. She pours diet Mountain Dew into a forty-nine-ounce tumbler, explaining it has more caffeine than other sodas and gives her a buzz. She slips on a neon-orange minidress ("I get a rush seeing my skeleton") and checks, as she does

NOTES

chronic (par. 4): long-term
criteria (par. 5): standards
folded (par. 5): closed
knapsack (par. 7): backpack
buzz (par. 8): feeling of slight intoxication
rush (par. 8): thrill

every day, to make sure her forearm fits in a circle formed by her thumb and finger. Then she spends an hour in a ritual typical of anorexics. She puts a cup of broccoli on a plate—the same plate every day—and places it on the couch under her arm, out of view. She slowly eats while watching *One Life to Live*, her favorite soap. She ponders yogurt and retrieves one from the freezer ("it's harder frozen, so you eat less"). By day's end she should have eaten 2,800 calories. But no one is watching over her, so she'll eat just 500.

9   The trailer is devoid of personal effects, save pictures of her family in heart-shaped frames. She points out a stuffed bunny left at her door by a college friend "who won't come in anymore because he can't stand to look at me." She notes that Prozac has helped her divorce herself from some elements of her past—for example, an obsessive neatness that kept her from allowing people to sit on her couch because "the cushions got squashed." But she still talks to her mother, an administrator at the university, four times a day.

10   Jayme says she used to go drinking every night with boyfriends until late last year, "when I lost the last forty pounds and scared them all away." Doesn't she want to date? "One of my main goals is to get married and have babies," she says brightly. But she hasn't had her period in eleven months, which causes her mother to say angrily, "I've come to accept the fact that I may never have grandchildren." Jayme has starved herself back into childhood—her skin is covered with lanugo, the hair infants are born with—and forward into old age. Her hair is thinning, her teeth are rotting, and the longer she goes without menstruating the more she risks bone decay. She is trapped between her future and her past.

11   Jayme and her twenty-three-year-old sister, Julie, grew up in Agra, an Oklahoma town that once had high hopes. Agra expected to become the site of a large freight center, and in the 1920s, a town of banks, saloons, cotton gins, and 1,000 residents sprouted in the middle of nowhere. But the freight center was located elsewhere, and by the 1970s, when Julie and Jayme were born into what had become the typical Agra home—a trailer—all that was left was a blind man's concession stand, three churches, a school with ten children per grade, and a population of 336. The only nightlife could be found in tin-shack bars. It was the smallest of small towns, the last place some might expect to find eating disorders, which have been tagged "rich kids' diseases."

12   But studies indicate that bulimia is most common among the lower classes and that anorexia occurs all over the United States. The drive to succeed can play a more crucial role in the disorders than class or location, doctors think. Certainly, the Porters had drive. The girls' father, Galen Porter, a construction supervisor who raised livestock and prided himself on "always having fun," even during his tour in Vietnam, served on the local and state school boards. When Agra made national news after a parent demanded that

NOTES

devoid (par. 9): empty

Prozac (par. 9): an antidepressant drug

bulimia (par. 12): Bulimia is characterized by episodes of bingeing and purging: gross overeating followed by self-induced vomiting, laxative abuse, and/or excessive exercise. This behavior is often carried out in secret and causes a great deal of shame. A bulimic's body weight is often normal or near normal.

the novel *The Color Purple* be taken off school shelves, Galen voted against censorship. He and his wife, Kay, sheltered their children from the more prohibitive local customs—which included a town church's demands that women stay at home, marry young, and never cut their hair—and encouraged them to succeed.

13   Succeed Julie and Jayme did. Agra's school had no arts and few sports programs, but it did have 4-H, Future Farmers of America, and Future Homemakers of America. Julie traveled the state with these organizations, winning speech contests while Jayme won sheep-showing contests. Both their bedrooms became shrines to achievement, their shelves stacked with trophies as tall as the pipes of a church organ. Both became one of only two in their grades to go to college.

14   Trouble hit when they were juniors in college. Their parents believe that for Julie, the discovery she wasn't going to be sorority president was the trigger: She lost forty pounds in two months and landed in a hospital weighing eighty-seven pounds. For Jayme, three years younger, her parents think it may have been the realization she hadn't excelled at anything since 4-H days. Both girls describe that period simply: "I had to be thinnest." As the last of their high school friends married, it was clear the sisters' ambition had spun out of control.

15   Julie was lucky. Although her mother's insurance policy picked up only $10,500 of the $73,000 bill for her nine-month stay at nearby Laureate Hospital, she was able to continue treatment because a bureaucratic error led Laureate to believe that welfare had taken up the slack. Even after the error was realized, Laureate let her stay on, swallowing more than $20,000.

16   Jayme was not so lucky. When she hit ninety pounds last January, Laureate refused to take her unless her parents paid the $35,000 balance on Julie's bill. Hearing of a program in Arizona called Remuda Ranch, Kay and Galen say they checked with a benefits coordinator who told them their insurance company, American Fidelity Assurance, would not provide more than $10,000. So they remortgaged their house to come up with an extra $23,000 to pay for sixty days. But Jayme would stay in Arizona only thirty-five days. Remuda told the Porters Jayme had to leave immediately because she was considered "noncompliant."

17   At home over the next few weeks, Jayme lost more weight. "There was no place else to go," says Kay. Then, suddenly, hope: Wichita's Dr. Pryor consented to treat Jayme first and fight the insurance company later. Pryor, who had been cured of anorexia at age fifteen, took one look at Jayme and checked her into the hospital's intensive care unit.

NOTES

prohibitive (par. 12): restrictive

shrines (par. 13): monuments

trigger (par. 14): cause

bureaucratic (par. 15): administrative

remortgaged their house (par. 16): borrowed money, giving the lender a claim to their house until the loan is repaid

noncompliant (par. 16): not cooperative

18   Jayme continued her downward spiral. Her weight dropped to sixty pounds, and she was in a state of hypothermia with a body temperature below 92 degrees. Within days, Pryor, fearing Jayme would die, called the family to her bedside. "She couldn't lift the sheets over herself," Kay recalls. "If she sat up, her heart would go to 180, then would slow to thirty-two beats a minute, and when she tried to get out of bed, it went off the charts. The nurses said you could see the outlines of her organs through her skin. Galen or I would sleep with her every night. We were terrified that if we left her she would die." Julie says she couldn't look at her sister: "I thought I'd be sick. I've seen skinny, skinny girls but nothing like that. She said she wanted a Mr. Potato Head, so I brought her one, but she couldn't even stick the little pieces in him."

19   Jayme pulled through with feeding tubes and was admitted to the psychiatric ward. She began sessions with Pryor. But after three weeks hope fizzled again. "They couldn't afford us, and we couldn't afford them anymore," says Pryor. Having racked up a $50,000 bill in Wichita, none of which American Fidelity paid, Jayme was released on April 23 weighing seventy-nine pounds.

20   Insurance company officials would not comment on the adequacy of their policy, but they did provide records showing that American Fidelity paid only $30,000 of the $180,000 in psychiatric bills hospitals charged them. Pryor, whose program has since closed, was upset she had to release Jayme. "We should be able to keep them in the hospital for weeks after they've achieved ideal body weight, so we can begin to control behavior," she says. "In 1994 the average inpatient stay of an anorexic here was twenty-one days—now it's two to four days. Patients are coming in so much sicker it's frightening. I've been notorious for forcing the hospital to swallow bills. That's no way to run a program. It's the craziest thing in the world."

21   In May, a month after Jayme was released, the nation's top eating disorders specialists gathered at the annual convention of the American Psychiatric Association in San Diego. They had a new problem. The National Alliance for the Mentally Ill was lobbying for bills in thirty-seven states that would require insurers to treat mental illnesses as seriously as physical illnesses. But NAMI hadn't recommended including eating disorders in any of the parity bills. So the doctors planned to take on both the insurance industry and their own profession. They would try to persuade NAMI to include eating disorders in its legislation.

22   "There's such bias," explained Illinois eating disorders expert Dr. Pat Santucci. "A congressman asked me, 'How am I supposed to convince a small-business man he has to pay for this girlie disease?'" NAMI postponed the meeting. About the bills, NAMI later explained, it can't risk combating the prejudices until the biology of these illnesses is better understood. Anorexia doctors can't afford many of their own patients, let alone their own lobbyists.

NOTES

hypothermia (par. 18): abnormally low body temperature
psychiatric ward (par. 19): unit of a hospital dedicated to helping people who are mentally ill
notorious (par. 20): well known (in an unfavorable way)
parity (par. 21): equivalency, equality
bias (par. 22): prejudice

They had to wait and watch as bills excluding eating disorders were passed in several states.

23   It's summer, and Jayme sits in her trailer, eyeing the clock like an alcoholic before cocktail hour. When it's time for her workout, she says, "Yes!" and leaps out of her slouch with arms and legs akimbo, like a puppet jerked to life.

24   No matter how anorexia begins, many doctors believe that starvation and compulsive exercising become addictive, and this is clearly true for Jayme. At the OSU gym, she sits in a machine that's twice as big as she is, working out with weights as heavy as she is, for nearly two hours. "I'm so strong," she says proudly.

25   Sixty miles away, in her Tulsa home, Julie flops into a chair, looking as puppetlike as her sister. But resemblances to Jayme end there. Julie received six months of intensive treatment—group therapy, psychotherapy, nutrition and body image class, AA, career counseling, twenty-four-hour monitoring—and it changed her life. She lost her rituals, lost her need to please the world. Her house is as cheerfully unkempt as Jayme's is spartan. She graduated from college in June and has developed a love she picked up at the hospital—art therapy. Now she's considering getting a master's.

26   Kay and Galen, $145,000 in debt, have seen strange times. They have lost faith in doctors, who keep telling them their daughters' health is a commodity they must purchase. "I'm scared stiff for any of us to get sick now," Kay says. Both shift from affection to disbelief when they speak of their girls, trying to recall which qualities which daughter has lost to her disease. The sisters say their parents can pretend their problems don't exist. And the family's dynamics have changed dramatically. Just when Julie and her parents should have been mending fences after her illness, Jayme began going through the same thing, distracting Kay and Galen's attention. Hurt, Julie rarely comes home. The lack of outside resources has made Jayme more dependent on her parents than ever, reflected in the sardonic tone she adopts when speaking to them. ("I'm just a manipulative little girl, aren't I, Mommy?" she says at one point, wrapping her arms around Kay's neck.) The girls, who have had to compete for attention and money, almost never speak to each other.

NOTES

akimbo (par. 23): bent

compulsive (par. 24): excessive

group therapy (par. 25): a form of therapy in which several clients, guided by a therapist (such as a psychologist or counselor), meet together to confront their personal difficulties

psychotherapy (par. 25): a form of therapy in which a therapist uses psychological methods to help a client overcome mental or emotional problems

nutrition and body image class (par. 25): a class designed to teach nutrition and develop an accurate and realistic image of what one's body is or should be like

AA (par. 25): Alcoholics Anonymous (a support group for people who wish to stop or have stopped drinking)

unkempt (par. 25): out of order

spartan (par. 25): rigidly ordered

commodity (par. 26): product

dynamics (par. 26): relationship

sardonic (par. 26): ironically humorous

27   The Porters were once a family of go-getters who worked and played hard together. Now Kay and Galen sometimes act like kids wondering where the fun has gone. The sisters often act like parents exasperated with the children; the parents, who lie in bed every night wondering what they did wrong, have been rendered as emotionally and financially helpless as their girls. The Porters are as trapped in their love for one another as they are trapped in the clutches of a disease—and a flawed health care system—they don't understand.

28   Julie will likely survive, which becomes evident when she talks about her weight. "Ninety-eight pounds," she says, though she doesn't like to admit it "because it's still too thin." Jayme, too, is afraid to reveal her weight, eighty-one pounds, but for a different reason: "It's not thin enough."

NOTE

exasperated (par. 27): out of patience

Heavy Judgment: A Sister Talks About the Pain of "Living Large"

Deborah Gregory

1   Thirteen years ago I was a model in Europe. I was cramped inside a tiny fitting room in Paris, and a couturier's purse-lipped assistant put a tape measure around my hips, then screamed, "Trop forte!" I didn't speak French, but I knew Madame wasn't delighted with my curvy proportions. The next day another designer called my agency and told them he wouldn't book me because I was too fat. The evidence in question: At five feet eleven inches tall I had the audacity to tip the scales at 140 pounds. Scandalous! It has taken me many years to forgive myself for not maintaining the rigid 125- to 130-pound model mandate—and to forgive the fashion industry for requiring mannequins to be paper-thin.

2   "Sashaying," however, isn't the only business practicing fat-cell-count discrimination: Monitoring women's size has become a weighty issue in the workplace. My favorite rationale is the film industry's hocus-pocus excuse that actresses need to be skinny because celluloid automatically adds ten pounds to their image. But, mind you, it's okay for hefty actors like Forest Whitaker (*A Rage in Harlem* and *The Crying Game*) to bare it all in love scenes. I have painfully discovered the extent of fat discrimination over the last ten years as I have vacillated between 140 and 235 pounds. I currently weigh around 200.

NOTES

couturier's (par. 1): fashion designer's
audacity (par. 1): nerve
scandalous (par. 1): shocking
mandate (par. 1): rule
rationale (par. 2): reason
hocus-pocus (par. 2): nonsense
celluloid (par. 2): film
vacillated (par. 2): moved back and forth

of over a million 25 miles from Hanibal. Every Friday and Saturday night, most of the Saints would meet between 8:00 and 8:30 and would go into Big Town. Big Town activities included drinking heavily in taverns or nightclubs, driving drunkenly through the streets, and committing acts of vandalism and playing pranks.

6   By midnight on Fridays and Saturdays, the Saints were usually thoroughly high, and one or two of them were often so drunk they had to be carried to the cars. Then the boys drove around town, calling obscenities to women and girls; occasionally trying (unsuccessfully so far as I could tell) to pick girls up; and driving recklessly through red lights and at high speeds with their lights out. Occasionally they played "chicken." One boy would climb out the back window of the car and across the roof to the driver's side of the car while the car was moving at high speed (between 40 and 50 miles an hour); then the driver would move over and the boy who had just crawled across the car roof would take the driver's seat.

7   Searching for "fair game" for a prank was the boys' principal activity after they left the tavern. The boys would drive alongside a foot patrolman and ask directions to some street. If the policeman leaned on the car in the course of answering the question, the driver would speed away, causing him to lose his balance. The Saints were careful to play this prank only in an area where they were not going to spend much time and where they could quickly disappear around a corner to avoid having their license plate number taken. Construction sites and road repair areas were the special province of the Saints' mischief. A soon-to-be-repaired hole in the road inevitably invited the Saints to remove lanterns and wooden barricades and put them in the car, leaving the hole unprotected. The boys would find a safe vantage point and wait for an unsuspecting motorist to drive into the hole. Often, though not always, the boys would go up to the motorist and commiserate with him about the dreadful way the city protected its citizenry.

8   Leaving the scene of the open hole and the motorist, the boys would then go searching for an appropriate place to erect the stolen barricade. An "appropriate place" was often a spot on a highway near a curve in the road where the barricade would not be seen by an oncoming motorist. The boys would wait to watch an unsuspecting motorist attempt to stop and (usually) crash into the wooden barricade. With saintly bearing the boys might offer help and understanding.

9   A stolen lantern might well find its way onto the back of a police car or hang from a street lamp. Once a lantern served as a prop for a reenactment of the "midnight ride of Paul Revere" until the "play," which was taking place at 2:00 A.M. in the center of a main street of Big Town, was interrupted by a police car several blocks away. The boys ran, leaving the lanterns on the street, and managed to avoid being apprehended. Abandoned houses, especially if they were located in out-of-the-way places, were fair game for

NOTES

province (par. 7): area of interest

vantage point (par. 7): place to view

commiserate (par. 7): sympathize

apprehended (par. 9): arrested

destruction and spontaneous vandalism. The boys would break windows, remove furniture to the yard and tear it apart, urinate on the walls, and scrawl obscenities inside.

10   Through all the pranks, drinking, and reckless driving, the boys managed miraculously to avoid being stopped by police. Only twice in two years was I aware that they had been stopped by a Big Town policeman. Once was for speeding (which they did every time they drove whether they were drunk or sober), and the driver managed to convince the policeman that it was simply an error. The second time they were stopped they had just left a nightclub and were walking through an alley. Aaron stopped to urinate and the boys began making obscene remarks. A foot patrolman came into the alley, lectured the boys, and sent them home. Before the boys got to the car, one began talking in a loud voice again. The policeman, who had followed them down the alley, arrested this boy for disturbing the peace and took him to the police station where the other Saints gathered. After paying a $5.00 fine, and with the assurance that there would be no permanent record of the arrest, the boy was released.

11   The boys had a spirit of frivolity and fun about their escapades. They did not view what they were engaged in as "delinquency," though it surely was by any reasonable definition of that word. They simply viewed themselves as having a little fun and who, they would ask, was really hurt by it? The answer had to be no one, although this fact remains one of the most difficult things to explain about the gang's behavior. Unlikely though it seems, in two years of drinking, driving, carousing, and vandalism, no one was seriously injured as a result of the Saints' activities.

The Saints in School

12   The Saints were highly successful in school. The average grade for the group was "B," with two of the boys having close to a straight "A" average. Almost all of the boys were popular, and many of them held offices in the school. One of the boys was vice president of the student body one year. Six of the boys played on athletic teams. At the end of their senior year, the student body selected ten seniors for special recognition as the "school wheels"; four of the ten were Saints. Teachers and school officials saw no problem with any of these boys and anticipated that they would all "make something of themselves."

13   How the boys managed to maintain this impression is surprising in view of their actual behavior in school. Their technique for covering truancy was so successful that teachers did not even realize that the boys were absent from school much of the time. Occasionally, of course, the system would backfire and then

NOTES

spontaneous (par. 9): unplanned
assurance (par. 10): promise
frivolity (par. 11): lightheartedness
escapades (par. 11): pranks, adventures
carousing (par. 11): drunken merrymaking

the boy was on his own. A boy who was caught would be most contrite, would plead guilty and ask for mercy. He inevitably got the mercy he sought.

14   Cheating on examinations was rampant, even to the point of orally communicating answers to exams as well as looking at one another's papers. Since none of the group studied, and since they were primarily dependent on one another for help, it is surprising that grades were so high. Teachers contributed to the deception in their admitted inclination to give these boys (and presumably others like them) the benefit of the doubt. When asked how the boys did in school, and when pressed on specific examinations, teachers might admit that they were disappointed in John's performance, but would quickly add that they "knew that he was capable of doing better," so John was given a higher grade than he had actually earned. How often this happened is impossible to know. During the time that I observed the group, I never saw any of the boys take homework home. Teachers may have been "understanding" very regularly.

15   One exception to the gang's generally good performance was Jerry, who had a "C" average in his junior year, experienced disaster the next year, and failed to graduate. Jerry had always been a little more nonchalant than the others about the liberties he took in school. Rather than wait for someone to come get him from class, he would offer his own excuse and leave. Although he probably did not miss any more class than most of the others in the group, he did not take the requisite pains to cover his absences. Jerry was the only Saint whom I ever heard talk back to a teacher. Although teachers often called him a "cut up" or a "smart kid," they never referred to him as a troublemaker or as a kid headed for trouble. It seems likely, then, that Jerry's failure his senior year and his mediocre performance his junior year were consequences of his not playing the game the proper way (possibly because he was disturbed by his parents' divorce). His teachers regarded him as "immature" and not quite ready to get out of high school.

The Police and the Saints

16   The local police saw the Saints as good boys who were among the leaders of the youth in the community. Rarely, the boys might be stopped in town for speeding or for running a stop sign. When this happened the boys were always polite, contrite, and pled for mercy. As in school, they received the mercy they asked for. None ever received a ticket or was taken into the precinct by the local police.

17   The situation in Big Town, where the boys engaged in most of their delinquency, was only slightly different. The police there did not know the boys at all, although occasionally the boys were stopped by a patrolman. Once they

NOTES

contrite (par. 13): remorseful, sorry

rampant (par. 14): limitless

inclination (par. 14): tendency

nonchalant (par. 15): unconcerned

requisite (par. 15): necessary

pains (par. 15): effort

were caught taking a lantern from a construction site. Another time they were stopped for running a stop sign, and on several occasions they were stopped for speeding. Their behavior was as before: contrite, polite, and penitent. The urban police, like the local police, accepted their demeanor as sincere. More important, the urban police were convinced that these were good boys just out for a lark.

The Roughnecks

18   Hanibal townspeople never perceived the Saints' high level of delinquency. The Saints were good boys who just went in for an occasional prank. After all, they were well dressed, well mannered and had nice cars. The Roughnecks were a different story. Although the two gangs of boys were the same age, and both groups engaged in an equal amount of wild-oat sowing, everyone agreed that the not-so-well-dressed, not-so-well-mannered, not-so-rich boys were heading for trouble. Townspeople would say, "You can see the gang members at the drugstore, night after night, leaning against the storefront (sometimes drunk) or slouching around inside buying cokes, reading magazines, and probably stealing old Mr. Wall blind. When they are outside and girls walk by, even respectable girls, these boys make suggestive remarks. Sometimes their remarks are downright lewd."

19   From the community's viewpoint, the real indication that these kids were in trouble was that they were constantly involved with the police. Some of them had been picked up for stealing, mostly small stuff, of course, "but still it's stealing small stuff that leads to big time crimes." "Too bad," people said. "Too bad that these boys couldn't behave like the other kids in town: stay out of trouble, be polite to adults, and look to their future."

20   The community's impression of the degrees to which this group of six boys (ranging in age from 16 to 19) engaged in delinquency was somewhat distorted. In some ways the gang was more delinquent than the community thought; in other ways, they were less. The fighting activities of the group were fairly readily and accurately perceived by almost everyone. At least once a month, the boys would get into some sort of fight, although most fights were scraps between members of the group or involved only one member of the group and some peripheral hanger-on. Only three times in the period of observation did the group fight together: once against a gang from across town, once against two blacks, and once against a group of boys from another school. For the first two fights the group went out "looking for trouble"— and they found it both times. The third fight followed a football game and began spontaneously with an argument on the football field between one of the Roughnecks and a member of the opposition's football team. Jack has a

NOTES

penitent (par. 17): regretful and apologetic

demeanor (par. 17): behavior

lark (par. 17): good time

distorted (par. 20): inaccurate

peripheral (par. 20): unimportant

particular propensity for fighting and was involved in most of the brawls. He was a prime mover of the escalation of arguments into fights.

21   More serious than fighting, had the community been aware of it, was theft. Although almost everyone was aware that the boys occasionally stole things, they did not realize the extent of the activity. Petty stealing was a frequent event for the Roughnecks. Sometimes they stole as a group and coordinated their efforts; other things they stole in pairs. Rarely did they steal alone.

22   The thefts ranged from very small things like paperback books, comics, and ball-point pens to expensive items like watches. The nature of the thefts varied from time to time. The gang would go through a period of systematically lifting items from automobiles or school lockers. Types of thievery varied with the whim of the gang. Some forms of thievery were more profitable than others, but all thefts were for profit, not just thrills. Roughnecks siphoned gasoline from cars as often as they had access to an automobile, which was not very often. Unlike the Saints, who owned their own cars, the Roughnecks would have to borrow their parents' cars, an event that occurred only eight or nine times a year. The boys claimed to have stolen cars for joy rides from time to time. Ron committed the most serious of the group's offenses. With an unidentified associate, the boy attempted to burglarize a gasoline station. Although this station had been robbed twice previously in the same month, Ron denied any involvement in either of the other thefts. When Ron and his accomplice approached the station, the owner was hiding in the bushes beside the station. He fired both barrels of a double-barreled shotgun at the boys. Ron was severely injured; the other boy ran away and was never caught. Though he remained in critical condition for several months, Ron finally recovered and served six months of the following year in reform school. Upon release from reform school, Ron was put back a grade in school, and began running around with a different gang of boys. The Roughnecks considered the new gang less delinquent than themselves, and during the following year Ron had no more trouble with the police.

23   The Roughnecks, then, engaged mainly in three types of delinquency: theft, drinking, and fighting. Although community members perceived that this gang of kids was delinquent, they mistakenly believed that their illegal activities were primarily drinking, fighting, and being a nuisance to passersby. Drinking was limited among the gang members, although it did occur, and theft was much more prevalent than anyone realized. Drinking would doubtless have been more prevalent had the boys had ready access to liquor. Since they rarely had automobiles at their disposal, they could not travel very far, and the bars in town would not serve them.

24   Most of the boys had little money, and this, too, inhibited their purchase of alcohol. Their major source of liquor was a local drunk who would buy them a fifth if they would give him enough extra to buy himself a pint of whiskey or a

NOTES

propensity (par. 20): tendency

systematically lifting (par. 22): methodically stealing

bottle of wine. The community's perception of drinking as prevalent stemmed from the fact that it was the most obvious delinquency the boys engaged in. When one of the boys had been drinking, even a casual observer seeing him on the comer would suspect that he was high.

25   There was a high level of mutual distrust and dislike between the Roughnecks and the police. The boys felt very strongly that the police were unfair and corrupt. Some evidence existed that the boys were correct in their perception.

26   The main source of the boys' dislike for the police undoubtedly stemmed from the fact that the police would sporadically harass the group. From the standpoint of the boys, these acts of occasional enforcement of the law were whimsical and uncalled for. It made no sense to them, for example, that the police would come to the corner occasionally and threaten them with arrest for loitering when the night before the boys had been out siphoning gasoline from cars and the police had been nowhere in sight. To the boys, the police were stupid on the one hand, for not being where they should have been and catching the boys in a serious offense, and unfair on the other hand, for trumping up "loitering" charges against them.

27   From the viewpoint of the police, the situation was quite different. They knew, with all the confidence necessary to be a policeman, that these boys were engaged in criminal activities. They knew this partly from occasionally catching them, mostly from circumstantial evidence ("the boys were around when those tires were slashed"), and partly because the police shared the view of the community in general that this was a bad bunch of boys. The best the police could hope to do was to be sensitive to the fact that these boys were engaged in illegal acts and arrest them whenever there was some evidence that they had been involved. Whether or not the boys had in fact committed a particular act in a particular way was not especially important. The police had a broader view: their job was to stamp out these kids' crimes; the tactics were not as important as the end result.

28   Over the period that the group was under observation, each member was arrested at least once. Several of the boys were arrested a number of times and spent at least one night in jail. While most were never taken to court, two of the boys were sentenced to six months' incarceration in boys' schools.

The Roughnecks in School

29   The Roughnecks' behavior in school was not particularly disruptive. During school hours they did not all hang around together, but tended instead to spend most of their time with one or two other members of the gang who were their special buddies. Although every member of the gang attempted to avoid school as much as possible, they were not particularly successful and

NOTES

prevalent (par. 24): frequent
sporadically (par. 26): periodically
whimsical (par. 26): inconsistent
trumping up (par. 26): making up
loitering (par. 26): hanging around a place for no obvious reason
circumstantial evidence (par. 27): evidence based on other events or circumstances

most of them attended school with surprising regularity. They considered school a burden—something to be gotten through with a minimum of conflict. If they were "bugged" by a particular teacher, it could lead to trouble. One of the boys, Al, once threatened to beat up a teacher and, according to the other boys, the teacher hid under a desk to escape him.

30   Teachers saw the boys the way the general community did, as heading for trouble, as being uninterested in making something of themselves. Some were also seen as being incapable of meeting the academic standards of the school. Most of the teachers expressed concern for this group of boys and were willing to pass them despite poor performance, in the belief that failing them would only aggravate the problem. The group of boys had a grade point average just slightly above "C." No one in the group failed either grade, and no one had better than a "C" average. They were very consistent in their achievement or, at least, the teachers were consistent in their perception of the boys' achievement.

31   Two of the boys were good football players. Herb was acknowledged to be the best player in the school, and Jack was almost as good. Both boys were criticized for their failure to abide by training rules, for refusing to come to practice as often as they should, and for not playing their best during practice. What they lacked in sportsmanship, they made up for in skill, apparently, and played every game no matter how poorly they had performed in practice or how many practice sessions they had missed.

Two Questions

32   Why did the community, the school, and the police react to the Saints as though they were good, upstanding, non delinquent youths with bright futures but to the Roughnecks as though they were tough, young criminals who were headed for trouble? Why did the Roughnecks and the Saints in fact have quite different careers after high school—careers which, by and large, lived up to the expectations of the community? The most obvious explanation for the differences in the community's and law enforcement agencies' reactions to the two gangs is that one group of boys was "more delinquent" than the other. Which group was more delinquent? The answer to this question will determine in part how we explain the differential responses to these groups by the members of the community and, particularly, by law enforcement and school officials.

33   In sheer number of illegal acts, the Saints were the more delinquent. They were truant from school for at least part of the day almost every day of the week. In addition, their drinking and vandalism occurred with surprising regularity. The Roughnecks, in contrast, engaged sporadically in delinquent episodes. While these episodes were frequent, they certainly did not occur on a daily or even a weekly basis.

34   The difference in frequency of offenses was probably caused by the Roughnecks' inability to obtain liquor and to manipulate legitimate excuses from

NOTES

bugged (par. 29): annoyed

differential (par. 32): unequal

sheer (par. 33): total

manipulate (par. 34): take advantage of

school. Since the Roughnecks had less money than the Saints, and teachers carefully supervised their school activities, the Roughnecks' hearts may have been as black as the Saints', but their misdeeds were not nearly as frequent.

35   There are really no clear-cut criteria by which to measure qualitative differences in antisocial behavior. The most important dimension is generally referred to as the "seriousness" of the offenses.

36   If seriousness encompasses the relative economic costs of delinquent acts, then some assessment can be made. The Roughnecks probably stole an average of about $5.00 worth of goods a week. Some weeks the figure was considerably higher, but these times must be balanced against long periods when almost nothing was stolen.

37   The Saints were more continuously engaged in delinquency but their acts were not for the most part costly to property. Only their vandalism and occasional theft of gasoline would so qualify. Perhaps once or twice a month they would siphon a tankful of gas. The other costly items were street signs, construction lanterns, and the like. All of these acts combined probably did not quite average $5.00 a week, partly because much of the stolen equipment was abandoned and presumably could be recovered. The difference in cost of stolen property between the two groups was trivial, but the Roughnecks probably had a slightly more expensive set of activities than did the Saints.

38   Another meaning of seriousness is the potential threat of physical harm to members of the community and to the boys themselves. The Roughnecks were more prone to physical violence; they not only welcomed an opportunity to fight; they went seeking it. In addition, they fought among themselves frequently. Although the fighting never included deadly weapons, it was still a menace, however minor, to the physical safety of those involved.

39   The Saints never fought. They avoided physical conflict both inside and outside the group. At the same time, though, the Saints frequently endangered their own and other people's lives. They did so almost every time they drove a car, especially if they had been drinking. Sober, their driving was risky; under the influence of alcohol it was horrendous. In addition, the Saints endangered the lives of others with their pranks. Street excavations left unmarked were a very serious hazard.

40   Evaluating the relative seriousness of the two gangs' activities is difficult. The community reacted as though the behavior of the Roughnecks was a problem, and they reacted as though the behavior of the Saints was not. But the members of the community were ignorant of the array of delinquent acts that characterized the Saints' behavior. Although concerned citizens were

NOTES

qualitative differences in (par. 35): differences in kinds of

encompasses (par. 36): includes

relative (par. 36): comparative

trivial (par. 37): insignificant

prone to (par. 38): likely to commit

menace (par. 38): danger

Street excavations (par. 39): Holes in the street (due to digging)

array (par. 40): range

unaware of much of the Roughnecks' behavior as well, they were much better informed about the Roughnecks' involvement in delinquency than they were about the Saints'.

Visibility

41   Differential treatment of the two gangs resulted in part because one gang was infinitely more visible than the other. This differential visibility was a direct function of the economic standing of the families. The Saints had access to automobiles and were able to remove themselves from the sight of the community. In as routine a decision as to where to go to have a milkshake after school, the Saints stayed away from the mainstream of community life. Lacking transportation, the Roughnecks could not make it to the edge of town. The center of town was the only practical place for them to meet since their homes were scattered throughout the town and any non central meeting place put an undue hardship on some members. Through necessity the Roughnecks congregated in a crowded area where everyone in the community passed frequently, including teachers and law enforcement officers. They could easily see the Roughnecks hanging around the drugstore.

42   The Roughnecks, of course, made themselves even more visible by making remarks to passersby and by occasionally getting into fights on the corner. Meanwhile, just as regularly, the Saints were either at the cafe on one edge of town or in the pool hall at the other edge of town. Without any particular realization that they were making themselves inconspicuous, the Saints were able to hide their time wasting. Not only were they removed from the mainstream of traffic, but they were almost always inside a building. On their escapades the Saints were also relatively invisible, since they left Hanibal and traveled to Big Town. Here, too, they were mobile, roaming the city, rarely going to the same area twice.

Demeanor

43   To the notion of visibility must be added the difference in the responses of group members to outside intervention with their activities. If one of the Saints was confronted with an accusing policeman, even if he felt he was truly innocent of a wrongdoing, his demeanor was apologetic and penitent. A Roughneck's attitude was almost the polar opposite. When confronted with a threatening adult authority, even one who tried to be pleasant, the Roughneck's hostility and disdain were clearly observable. Sometimes he might attempt to put up a veneer of respect, but it was thin and was not accepted as sincere by the authority. School was no different from the community at large. The Saints could manipulate the system by feigning compliance with

NOTES

congregated (par. 41): gathered

inconspicuous (par. 42): unnoticeable

polar opposite (par. 43): exact opposite

disdain (par. 43): lack of respect

veneer (par. 43): appearance

feigning (par. 43): faking

the school norms. The availability of cars at school meant that once free from the immediate sight of the teacher, the boys could disappear rapidly. And this escape was well enough planned that no administrator or teacher was nearby when the boys left. A Roughneck who wished to escape for a few hours was in a bind. If it were possible to get free from class, downtown was still a mile away, and even if he arrived there, he was still very visible. Truancy for the Roughnecks meant almost certain detection, while the Saints enjoyed almost complete immunity from sanctions.

Bias

44   Community members were not aware of the transgressions of the Saints. Even if the Saints had been less discreet, their favorite delinquencies would have been perceived as less serious than those of the Roughnecks.

45   In the eyes of the police and school officials, a boy who drinks in an alley and stands intoxicated on the street corner is committing a more serious offense than is a boy who drinks to inebriation in a nightclub or a tavern and drives around afterwards in a car. Similarly, a boy who steals a wallet from a store will be viewed as having committed a more serious offense than a boy who steals a lantern from a construction site. Perceptual bias also operates with respect to the demeanor of the boys in the two groups when they are confronted by adults. It is not simply that adults dislike the posture affected by boys of the Roughneck ilk; more important is the conviction that the posture adopted by the Roughnecks is an indication of their devotion and commitment to deviance as a way of life. The posture becomes a cue, just as the type of the offense is a cue, to the degree to which the known transgressions are indicators of the youths' potential for other problems.

46   Visibility, demeanor, and bias are surface variables which explain the day-to-day operations of the police. Why do these surface variables operate as they do? Why did the police choose to disregard the Saints' delinquencies while breathing down the backs of the Roughnecks?

47   The answer lies in the class structure of American society and the control of legal institutions by those at the top of the class structure. Obviously, no representative of the upper class drew up the operational chart for the police, which led them to look in the ghettos and on street comers—which led them to see the demeanor of lower-class youth as troublesome and that of upper-middle-class youth as tolerable. Rather, the procedures simply developed from—experience—experience with irate and influential upper-middle-class

NOTES

bias (title above par. 44): prejudice

transgressions (par. 44): wrongdoings

discreet (par. 44): careful

inebriation (par. 45): drunkenness

perceptual bias (par. 45): seeing what one wants to see

posture (par. 45): attitude

ilk (par. 45): kind

surface variables (par. 46): the conditions

irate (par. 47): furious

parents insisting that their son's vandalism was simply a prank and his drunkenness only a momentary "sowing of wild oats" experience with cooperative or indifferent, powerless, lower-class parents who acquiesced to the law's definition of their son's behavior.

Adult Careers of the Saints and the Roughnecks

48   The community's confidence in the potential of the Saints and the Roughnecks apparently was justified. If anything, the community members underestimated the degree to which these youngsters would turn out "good" or "bad."

49   Seven of the eight members of the Saints went on to college immediately after high school. Five of the boys graduated from college in four years. The sixth one finished college after two years in the army, and the seventh spent four years in the air force before returning to college and receiving a B.A. degree. Of these seven college graduates, three went on for advanced degrees. One finished law school and is now active in state politics, one finished medical school and is practicing near Hanibal, and one boy is now working for a Ph.D. The other four college graduates entered sub-managerial, managerial, or executive training positions with larger firms.

50   The only Saint who did not complete college was Jerry. Jerry had failed to graduate from high school with the other Saints. During his second senior year, after the other Saints had gone on to college, Jerry began to hang around with what several teachers described as a "rough crowd"—the gang that was heir apparent to the Roughnecks. At the end of his second senior year, when he did graduate from high school, Jerry took a job as a used car salesman, got married, and quickly had a child. Although he made several abortive attempts to go to college by attending night school, when I last saw him (ten years after high school) Jerry was unemployed and had been living on unemployment for almost a year. His wife worked as a waitress.

51   Some of the Roughnecks have lived up to community expectations. A number of them were headed for trouble. A few were not.

52   Jack and Herb were the athletes among the Roughnecks and their athletic prowess paid off handsomely. Both boys received unsolicited athletic scholarships to college. After Herb received his scholarship (near the end of his senior year), he apparently did an about-face. His demeanor became very similar to that of the Saints. Although he remained a member in good standing of the Roughnecks, he stopped participating in most activities and did not hang out on the corner as often.

53   Jack did not change. If anything, he became more prone to fighting. He even made excuses for accepting the scholarship. He told the other gang members that the school had guaranteed him a "C" average if he would come

NOTES

acquiesced (par. 47): gave in
heir apparent to (par. 50): the apparent successor or replacement
abortive (par. 50): unsuccessful
handsomely (par. 52): very well
unsolicited (par. 52): unrequested
did an about-face (par. 52): changed his attitude

to play football—an idea that seems far-fetched, even in this day of highly competitive recruiting.

54   During the summer after graduation from high school, Jack attempted suicide by jumping from a tall building. The jump would certainly have killed most people trying it, but Jack survived. He entered college in the fall and played four years of football. He and Herb graduated in four years, and both are teaching and coaching in high schools. They are married and have stable families. If anything, Jack appears to have a more prestigious position in the community than does Herb, though both are well respected and secure in their positions.

55   Two of the boys never finished high school. Tommy left at the end of his junior year and went to another state. That summer he was arrested and placed on probation on a manslaughter charge. Three years later he was arrested for murder; he pleaded guilty to second degree murder and is serving a 30 year sentence in the state penitentiary. Al, the other boy who did not finish high school, also left the state in his senior year. He is serving a life sentence in a state penitentiary for first degree murder. Wes is a small-time gambler. He finished high school and "bummed around." After several years he made contact with a bookmaker who employed him as a runner. Later he acquired his own area and has been working it ever since. His position among the bookmakers is almost identical to the position he had in the gang; he is always around but no one is really aware of him. He makes no trouble and he does not get into any. Steady, reliable, capable of keeping his mouth closed, he plays the game by the rules, even though the game is an illegal one.

56   That leaves only Ron. Some of his former friends reported that they had heard he was "driving a truck up north," but no one could provide any concrete information.

Reinforcement

57   The community responded to the Roughnecks as boys in trouble, and the boys agreed with that perception. Their pattern of deviancy was reinforced, and breaking away from it became increasingly unlikely. Once the boys acquired an image of themselves as deviants, they selected new friends who affirmed that self-image. As that self conception became more firmly entrenched, they also became willing to try new and more extreme deviances. With their growing alienation came freer expression of disrespect and hostility for representatives of the legitimate society. This disrespect increased the community's negativism, perpetuating the entire process of commitment to deviance. Lack of a commitment to deviance works the same way. In either

NOTES

far-fetched (par. 53): unlikely

prestigious (par. 54): honored

bookmaker (par. 55): person who takes bets

runner (par. 55): a bookmaker's messenger or collector

self conception (par. 57): self-image

entrenched (par. 57): established

perpetuating (par. 57): continuing

case, the process will perpetuate itself unless some event (like a scholarship to college or a sudden failure) external to the established relationship intervenes. For two of the Roughnecks (Herb and Jack), receiving college athletic scholarships created new relations and culminated in a break with the established pattern of deviance. In the case of one of the Saints (Jerry), his parents' divorce and his failing to graduate from high school changed some of his other relations. Being held back in school for a year and losing his place among the Saints had sufficient impact on Jerry to alter his self-image and virtually to assure that he would not go on to college as his peers did. Although the experiments of life can rarely be reversed, it seems likely in view of the behavior of the other boys who did not enjoy this special treatment by the school that Jerry, too, would have "become something" had he graduated as anticipated. For Herb and Jack outside intervention worked to their advantage; for Jerry it was his undoing.

58   Selective perception and labeling—finding, processing, and punishing some kinds of criminality and not others—means that visible, poor, non-mobile, outspoken, undiplomatic "tough" kids will be noticed, whether their actions are seriously delinquent or not. Other kids, who have established a reputation for being bright (even though underachieving), disciplined, and involved in respectable activities, who are mobile and moneyed, will be invisible when they deviate from sanctioned activities. They'll sow their wild oats—perhaps even wider and thicker than their lower-class cohorts—but they won't be noticed. When it's time to leave adolescence, most will follow the expected path, settling into the ways of the middle class, remembering fondly the delinquent but unnoticed fling of their youth. The Roughnecks and others like them may turn around, too. It is more likely that their noticeable deviance will have been so reinforced by police and community that their lives will be effectively channeled into careers consistent with their adolescent background.

NOTES

relations (par. 57): connections

culminated (par. 57): ended

sanctioned (par. 58): approved

cohorts (par. 58): peers, people of the same age

fling (par. 58): carefree fun

Textbook
Chapters

Presidency in Crisis

Policies of the Nixon,
Ford, and Carter
Administrations
1968–1980

Joseph R. Conlin

from
**The American Past:
A Survey of American History**

Seventh Edition

49

PRESIDENCY IN CRISIS

The Nixon, Ford, and Carter Administrations 1968–1980

White House Photography

In a country where there is no hereditary throne nor hereditary aristocracy, an office raised far above all other offices offers too great a stimulus to ambition. This glittering prize, always dangling before the eyes of prominent statesmen, has a power stronger than any dignity under a European crown to lure them from the path of straightforward consistency.

James Lord Bryce

Americans expect their presidents to do what no monarch by Divine Right could ever do—resolve for them all the contradictions and complexities of life.

Robert T. Hartmann

THE HEROES OF Greek myth were constantly pursuing Proteus, the herdsman of the seas, for he could foresee the future and, if captured, had to reveal what he knew. Proteus was rarely caught. He also had the power to assume the shape of any creature, enabling him to wriggle out of his pursuers' grasp.

Richard Milhous Nixon, his enemies said, was never quite captured because he was always changing his shape. John Kennedy said that Nixon pretended to be so many different people that he had forgotten who he was. Liberals called him "Tricky Dicky." At several turns of his career, even his Republican boosters were constrained to assure Americans that the "Old Nixon" was no more; it was a "New Nixon" who was running for office.

The "Real Nixon," like the real Proteus, remained elusive and enigmatic to the end. Senator Barry Goldwater said that Richard Nixon was "the most complete loner I've ever known."

THE NIXON PRESIDENCY

Nixon is a compelling historical figure. He lacked the personal qualities thought essential to success in late-twentieth-century politics: He was not physically attractive; he lacked social grace, wit, and "charisma." No one ever said of him, "He's a nice guy." Nixon was shy; his manner was furtive. He disguised his discomfort in front of a crowd by willing it, by changing his shape.

Odd Duck

The liberals' dislike of Nixon had the intensity of a hatred, but those who hated the liberals did not love Nixon. President

Affirmative Action

Originally, as Lyndon Johnson defined it in coining the phrase, "affirmative action" was an admonition to employers and universities to be aggressive in recruiting members of racial minorities and women as a way of righting past wrongs. By the 1980s, affirmative action had come to mean giving preference in employment and admission to educational institutions to women, African Americans, Hispanics, Indians, and Pacific Islanders. As such, by 1990 it was a defining position of the "politically correct," especially academics and university administrators. They were so determined to preserve preferences in admissions policies that when courts and referenda struck down their affirmative action programs, they contrived convoluted schemes by which to preserve racial preferences while adhering to the letter of the law. (Before 2000, the numbers of white women in virtually all educational programs made them victims, rather than beneficiaries, of affirmative action.)

Affirmative action never had widespread support. Public opinion polls revealed that a majority of every group affected by it, both groups discriminated against (whites, Asian Americans, males) and those that benefited (African Americans, Hispanics, women) opposed race- or gender-based preferences. Because Democratic candidates for public office could not afford to oppose affirmative action vigorously (they needed the "politically correct" voters), the issue probably contributed to the decline of the party at the turn of the century.

Ironically, Republicans, not Democrats, were responsible for the reinterpretation of affirmative action to mean preferential treatment. In the Nixon administration, federal agencies were instructed that they were to favor businesses owned by members of minority groups when doling out federal contracts. Republican political strategists understood that in helping to create more wealthy African American and Hispanic businesspeople, they were creating voters and campaign contributors for whom Republican probusiness policies trumped Democratic sentiments based on race and gender. The percentage of African Americans voting Republican remained small during the 1990s but grew annually as the numbers of wealthy and middle-class black people increased. Affirmative action never affected voting patterns among women; women remained just about evenly divided between the two major parties, as they had been since 1920.

Eisenhower came within a hair of dumping him as his running mate in 1952 and considered replacing him in 1956. In 1960, when Nixon was running for president by emphasizing his experience, Ike humiliated him by saying he was unable to recall an instance in which Nixon contributed to an important decision.

The right-wing Republicans Nixon served well for two decades accepted his leadership without trusting him. When Nixon faced the premature end of his presidency, aides who owed their careers to him stumbled over one another in their haste to turn on him. All was forgiven at his funeral in 1994: Eulogists focused on his achievements, which were numerous, one momentous. Aside from his daughters, however, no

one at the memorial ceremonies at Nixon's boyhood home in Whittier, California, spoke of him with affection.

Richard Nixon clawed his way from a middle-class background in southern California to the top of the heap through hard work and the tenacious bite of a pit bull. Although he overstated it in his autobiographical *Six Crises,* he overcame formidable obstacles. If the self-made Horatio Alger boy is an American hero, Nixon belongs in the pantheon, for he was all pluck and little luck. Whatever else historians may say of Richard Nixon, he earned everything he ever got.

Political Savvy

President Nixon had little interest in domestic matters. He believed that "the country could run itself domestically without a president." He left all but the most important decisions to two young White House aides, H. R. Haldeman and John Ehrlichman. With a studied arrogance that amused them, Haldeman and Ehrlichman insulated Nixon from Congress and sometimes from his cabinet. They were themselves unpopular. Like Nixon, they would have few friends when the roof collapsed on the administration.

Politicking, which Nixon never enjoyed, he left to Vice President Spiro T. Agnew, a former governor of Maryland whom Nixon named to the ticket to attract the blue-collar and ethnic voters whom third-party George Wallace was trying to seduce. Agnew was an energetic campaigner and relished his role as Nixon's hit man. He stormed around the country delighting Republican conservatives by flailing antiwar students and the weak-willed, overpaid educators who indulged them in their disruptive activities. He excoriated liberal Supreme Court justices and the news media. Agnew was fond of tongue-twisting alliteration. His masterpiece was "nattering nabobs of negativism," that is, journalists.

Agnew's liberal baiting provided Nixon with a superb smoke screen, for, despite his many denunciations of big-spending liberal government, the president had no interest in dismantling the bureaucracies the Great Society had created. His only major modification of Lyndon Johnson's welfare state was the "New Federalism": turning federal revenues over to the states so that they could run social programs. The New Federalism actually increased the overall size of the nation's government bureaucracies and the inefficiency and waste inevitable in large organizations.

On other fronts, Nixon might as well have been a Democrat. He sponsored a scheme for welfare reform, the Family Assistance Plan, that was to provide a flat annual payment to poor households if their breadwinners registered with employment agencies. (It failed in Congress.) When, in 1971, Nixon worried that a jump in inflation might threaten his reelection the following year, he slapped on wage and price controls, a Republican anathema since World War II.

And yet, Democrats could not gloat, and few Republicans yelped. Nixon understood that the people who ran his party cared only about power and business-friendly government. The grassroots "conservatives" he called the "silent majority" were largely indifferent, or even favorable, toward liberal economic policies. They were repelled by the social

4 Cultural Diversity

there is considerable cultural variability *between* societies and sometimes *within* the same society. *Subcultures* and *countercultures* account for some of the complexity within a society.

SUBCULTURES

A **subculture** is a group or category of people whose distinctive ways of thinking, feeling, and acting differ somewhat from those of the larger society. A subculture is part of the larger, dominant culture but has particular values, beliefs, perspectives, lifestyle, or language. Members of subcultures often live in the same neighborhoods, associate with each other, have close personal relationships, and marry others who are similar to themselves.

One example of a subculture is college students. At residential campuses, most college students wear similar clothing, eat similar food, participate in similar recreational activities, and often date each other. Whether students live in campus housing or commute, they share a similar vocabulary that includes words like *syllabus,* *incomplete grade, dean's list,* and *core courses.* Many students are also members of other campus subcultures as well: sororities and fraternities, sports teams, clubs, or honor societies. In their home communities, college students are members of other subcultures, such as religious, political, and ethnic groups.

Whether we realize it or not, most of us are members of numerous subcultures. Subcultures reflect a variety of characteristics, interests, or activities:

- *Ethnicity* (Irish, Polish Americans, Vietnamese, Russians)
- *Religion* (Catholics, evangelical Christians, atheists, Mormons)
- *Politics* (Maine Republicans, Southern Democrats, independents, libertarians)
- *Sex and gender* (gay men, lesbians, transsexuals)
- *Age* (elderly widows, kindergarteners, middle schoolers)
- *Occupation* (surgeons, teachers, prostitutes, police officers, truck drivers)
- *Music and art* (jazz aficionados, opera buffs, art lovers)
- *Physical disability* (people who are deaf, quadriplegic, or blind)
- *Social class* (Boston Brahmin, working poor, middle class, jet set)
- *Recreation* (mountain bikers, bingo or poker players, motorcycle riders)

Some subcultures retreat from the dominant culture to preserve their beliefs and values. The Amish, for example, have created self-sustaining economic units, travel locally by horse and buggy, conduct religious services in their homes, make their own clothes, and generally shun modern conveniences such as electricity and phones. Despite their self-imposed isolation, the Amish have been affected by the dominant U.S. culture. They traditionally worked in agriculture, but as farming became less self-sustaining, many began small businesses that produce quilts, wood and leather products, and baked goods for tourists.

To fit in, members of most ethnic and religious subcultures adapt to the

subculture a group or category of people whose distinctive ways of thinking, feeling, and acting differ somewhat from those of the larger society.

Some analysts describe the popular television program **The Simpsons** *as countercultural because it ridicules the media's shallowness, portrays government in a cynical light, mocks indifferent or incompetent teachers and administrators, makes fun of stereotyping Asians who manage convenience stores, and scoffs at bungling and greedy law enforcement officers (Reeves 1999; Cantor 2001).*

20TH CENTURY FOX/THE KOBAL COLLECTION/GROENING, MATT/Picture Desk

larger society. Some Chinese restaurants have changed their menus to accommodate the average American's taste for sweet-and-sour dishes but list more authentic food on a separate, Chinese-language menu. Fearing discrimination, some Muslim girls and women don't wear a *hijab,* or head scarf, to classes. And those who don't abide by religious laws (modest dress, a ban on alcohol, prayer five times a day, and limited interaction with the opposite sex) often feel pressure from their Muslim peers to conform to such orthodox practices (McMurtrie 2001).

In many instances, subcultures arise because of technological or other societal changes. With the emergence of the Internet, for example, subcultures arose that identified themselves as hackers, techies, or computer geeks.

COUNTERCULTURES

Unlike a subculture, a **counterculture** deliberately opposes and consciously rejects some of the basic beliefs, values, and norms of the dominant culture. Countercultures usually emerge when people believe they cannot achieve their goals within the existing society. As a result, such groups develop values and practices that run counter to those of the established society. Some countercultures are small and informal, but others have millions of members and are highly organized, like religious militants (see Chapter 15).

Most countercultures do not engage in illegal activities. During the 1960s, for example, social movements such as feminism, civil rights, and gay rights organized protests against mainstream views but stayed within the law. However, some countercultures are violent and extremist, such as the 888 active hate groups across the United States (see *Figure 3.3*), who intimidate ethnic groups and gays. There have been instances where counterculture

members have clearly violated laws: Some skinheads have murdered gays; antigovernment militia adherents bombed a federal building in Oklahoma, killing dozens of adults and children; and anti-abortion advocates have murdered physicians and bombed abortion clinics

ETHNOCENTRISM

When President Bush visited Queen Elizabeth II in England in 2003, he brought with him five of his personal chefs. The Queen was offended because she has a large staff of excellent cooks ("Bush's Cooks . . . " 2003). Was President Bush being ethnocentric?

Ethnocentrism is the belief that one's culture and way of life are superior to those of other groups. This attitude leads people to view other cultures as inferior, wrong, backward, immoral, or barbaric. Countries and people display their ethnocentrism in many ways. During the nineteenth and twentieth centuries, there was rampant anti-immigrant sentiment toward people coming from Ireland, Poland, and other European countries. The Chinese Exclusion Act of 1882 barred Chinese immigrants and the Immigration Act of 1924 used quotas to limit Italian and Jewish immigration.

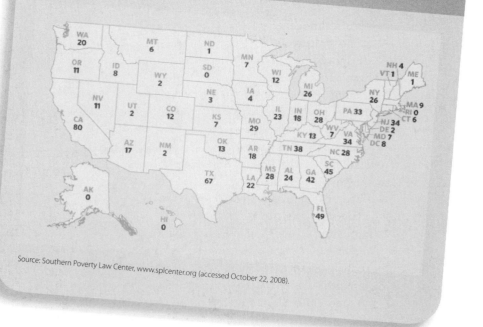

FIGURE 3.3
Active Hate Groups in the United States: 2008

Source: Southern Poverty Law Center, www.splcenter.org (accessed October 22, 2008).

Because people internalize their culture and take it for granted, they may be hostile toward other cultures. Each group tends to see its way of life as the best and the most natural. Some of my black students argue that it's impossible for African Americans to be ethnocentric because they suffer much prejudice and discrimination. *Any* group can be ethnocentric, however (Rose 1997). An immigrant from Nigeria who assumes that all native-born African Americans are lazy and criminal is just as ethnocentric as a native-born African American who assumes that all Nigerians are arrogant and "uppity."

Ethnocentrism can sometimes be functional. Pride in one's country promotes loyalty and cultural unity. When children learn their country's national anthem and customs, they have a sense of belonging. Ethnocentrism also reinforces conformity and maintains stability. Members of a society become committed to their particular values and customs and transmit them to the next generation. As a result, life is (generally) orderly and predictable.

Ethnocentrism has its benefits, but it is usually dysfunctional. Viewing others as inferior generates hatred, discrimination, and conflict. Many of the recent wars, such as those in the former Yugoslavia and Rwanda (Africa), and the ongoing battles between Palestinians and Israelis reflect religious, ethnic, or political intolerance toward subgroups (see Chapter 15 and online Chapter 18). Thus, ethnocentrism discourages intergroup understanding and cooperation.

CULTURAL RELATIVISM

The opposite of ethnocentrism is **cultural relativism**, a belief that no culture is better than another and that a culture should be judged by its own standards. Most Japanese mothers stay home with their children, while many American mothers are employed outside the home. Is one practice better than another? No. Because Japanese fathers are expected to be the breadwinners, it's common for many Japanese women to be homemakers. In the United States, in contrast, many mothers are single heads of households who have to work to provide for themselves and their children. Also, economic recessions and the loss of many high-paying jobs in the United States have catapulted many middle-class women into the job market to help support their families (see Chapters 10, 12, and 13). Thus, Japanese and American parenting may be different, but one culture isn't better or worse than the other.

An appreciation of cultural relativism is practical and productive. Businesspeople and other travelers can overcome cultural barriers and improve communication if they understand and respect other cultures. However, respecting other cultures' customs and traditions does not require that we remain mute when countries violate human rights, practice female infanticide, or sell young girls for prostitution.

> **cultural relativism** the belief that no culture is better than another and that a culture should be judged by its own standards.
>
> **multiculturalism** *(cultural pluralism)* the coexistence of several cultures in the same geographic area, without any one culture dominating another.
>
> **popular culture** the beliefs, practices, activities, and products that are widely shared among a population in everyday life.

MULTICULTURALISM

Multiculturalism (sometimes called *cultural pluralism*) refers to the coexistence of several cultures in the same geographic area, without one culture dominating another. Many applaud multiculturalism because it encourages intracultural dialogue (for example, U.S. schools offering programs and courses in African American, Latino, Arabic, and Asian studies). Supporters hope that emphasizing multiculturalism—especially in academic institutions and the workplace—will decrease ethnocentrism, racism, sexism, and other forms of discrimination.

Despite its benefits, not everyone is enthusiastic about multiculturalism. Not learning the language of the country in which one lives and works, for instance, can be isolating and create on-the-job miscommunication, tension, and conflict. Some also feel that multiculturalism can destroy a country's national traditions, heritage, and identity because ethnic and religious subcultures may not support the dominant culture's values and beliefs (Watson 2000; Skerry 2002).

A major component of culture is popular culture. Popular culture has enormous significance in many contemporary societies.

5 Popular Culture

Popular culture refers to beliefs, practices, activities, and products that are widely shared within a population in everyday life. Popular culture includes television, music, magazines, radio, advertising, sports, hobbies, fads, fashions, and movies

The incidence of obesity among American children and teenagers has more than tripled, rising from 5 percent in the 1960s to almost 17 percent by 2006 (Ogden et al. 2008). There are many reasons for the increase, but physicians and researchers lay much of the blame on popular culture, especially the advertising industry. Marketers in the United States spend an estimated

PRNewsFoto/Burger King Corporation/AP Photo

$10 billion a year to market products to children. Much of the advertising, particularly on television, uses cartoon characters like SpongeBob SquarePants and Scooby-Doo to sell sugary cereal, cookies, candy, and other high-calorie snacks (Institute of Medicine 2006; Strasburger et al. 2006). In contrast, many European countries forbid advertising on children's television programs.

---

mass media forms of communication designed to reach large numbers of people.

as well as the food we eat, the gossip we share, and the jokes we pass along to others. People produce and consume popular culture: They are not simply passive receptacles but influence popular culture by what they buy, how they spend their leisure time, and how they express themselves.

THE IMPACT OF POPULAR CULTURE

Popular culture can have positive and negative effects on our everyday lives. Most people do not believe everything they read or see on television but weigh the merit and credibility of much of the content. Further, in a national study of high school students, 46 percent of the teenagers identified a family member as their role model and another 16 percent chose a friend or a family friend rather than an entertainer or a sports figure (Hebert and Rivlin 2002). Thus, many young people aren't star-struck.

Most of us are highly influenced, nonetheless, by a popular culture that is largely controlled and manipulated to some extent by newspapers and magazines, television, movies, music, and ads (see Chapter 4). These **mass media**, or forms of communication designed to reach large numbers of people, have enormous power in shaping public perceptions and opinions. Let's look at a few examples.

Newspapers and Magazines

How accurate is the information we get from the mass media? Even though crime has decreased in the United States in recent years, newspapers and magazines have increased the amount of space they devote to covering violence. School violence is always a popular topic, even though schools are safer now than they were almost 20 years ago (Dinkes et al. 2007). In addition, the coverage can be deceptive. For example, a study of school violence concluded that six of the most influential newspapers (including the *New York Times, Washington Post,* and *Los Angeles Times*) portray violence in rural/suburban and urban schools differently. The newspapers were much less likely to print stories about shootings in urban school systems even though they occur twelve times more often than in rural schools. Violence in rural and suburban schools gets more coverage because many Americans have a stereotypical picture of rural life as peaceful and tranquil (Menifield et al. 2001).

Advertising and Commercials

The average American views 3,000 ads per day and at least 40,000 commercials on television per year, unless she or he has a service, such as TiVo, that skips commercials when recording television programs (Kilbourne 1999; Strasburger et al. 2006). We are constantly deluged with advertising in newspapers and magazines, on television and radio, in movie theaters, on billboards and the sides of buildings, on public transportation, and on the Internet. My Sunday newspaper comes in two big plastic bags, but about 80 percent of the content is advertising.

Many of my students, who claim that they "don't pay any attention to ads," come to class wearing branded apparel: Budweiser caps, Adidas sweatshirts, Old Navy T-shirts, or Nike footwear. A national study of people aged 15 to 26 years concluded that—regardless of gender, ethnicity, and educational level—exposure to alcohol advertising contributed to increased drinking. Those who saw more ads for alcoholic beverages tended to drink more and those who remembered the ads drank the most (Snyder et al. 2006).

Much mass media content is basically marketing. Many of the *Dr. Phil* shows plug his books and other products, as well as those of his wife and older son. Much of the content on television morning shows and MTV has become "a kind of sophisticated infomercial" (O'Donnell 2007:30). For example, a third of the content on morning shows (like the *Early Show* on CBS, the *Today Show* on NBC, and *Good Morning America* on ABC) is essentially selling something (a book, music, a movie, or another television program) that the corporation owns. One of the most lucrative alliances is between Hollywood and toy manufacturers. (See Chapter 4.)

And, according to some scholars, the U.S. mass media have reduced competition at home and have expanded cultural imperialism abroad.

CULTURAL IMPERIALISM

In **cultural imperialism**, the cultural values and products of one society influence or dominate those of another. Many countries complain that U.S. cultural imperialism displaces authentic local culture and results in cultural loss. The United States established the Internet, a global media network. The Internet uses mainly English and is heavily saturated with American advertising and popular culture (Louw 2001).

For example, a study of over 1,300 teenagers in 12 countries found that many enjoy American movies, television, celebrities, entertainers, and popular music. On the downside, images in U.S. mass media lead teens around the world to believe that Americans are extremely violent, criminal, and sexually immoral. U.S. news media, similarly, emphasize crime, corruption, sex, and violence far beyond what the ordinary American experiences on a daily basis (DeFleur and DeFleur 2003).

6 Cultural Change and Technology

" adio has no future" (Lord Kelvin, Scottish mathematician and physicist, 1897).

- "Everything that can be invented has been invented" (Charles H. Duell, U.S. commissioner of patents, 1899).

- "Television won't be able to hold on to any market it captures after the first six months. People will soon get tired of staring at a plywood box every night" (Darryl F. Zanuck, head of Hollywood's 20th Century-Fox studio, 1946).

- "There is no reason for any individual to have a computer in their home" (Kenneth Olsen, president and founder of Digital Equipment Corp., 1977).

Despite these predictions, radio, television, computers, and other new technologies have triggered major cultural changes around the world. This section examines why cultures persist, how and why they change, and what occurs when technology changes faster than cultural values, laws, and attitudes do.

CULTURAL PERSISTENCE: WHY CULTURES ARE STABLE

In many ways, culture is a conservative force. As you saw earlier, values, norms, and language are transmitted from generation to generation. Such **cultural integration**, or the consistency of various aspects of society, promotes order and stability. Even when new behaviors and beliefs emerge, they commonly adapt to existing ones. New immigrants, for example, may speak their native language at home and celebrate their own holy days, but they are expected to gradually absorb the new country's values, obey its civil and criminal codes, and adopt its national language. Life would be chaotic and unpredictable without such cultural integration.

CULTURAL DYNAMICS: WHY CULTURES CHANGE

Cultural stability is important, but all societies change over time. Some of the major reasons for cultural change include diffusion, invention and innovation, discovery, external pressures, and changes in the physical environment.

Diffusion

A culture may change due to *diffusion*, the process through which components of culture spread from one society to another. Such borrowing may have occurred

> **cultural imperialism** the influence or domination of the cultural values and products of one society over those of another.
>
> **cultural integration** the consistency of various aspects of society that promotes order and stability.

so long ago that the members of a society consider their culture to be entirely their own creation. However, anthropologist Ralph Linton (1964) has estimated that 90 percent of the elements of any culture are a result of diffusion (see *Figure 3.4*).

Diffusion can be direct and conscious, occurring through trade, tourism, immigration, intermarriage, or the invasion of one country by another. Diffusion can also be indirect and largely unconscious, as in the Internet transmissions that zip around the world.

Invention and Innovation

Cultures change because people are continually finding new ways of doing things. Invention, the process of creating new things, brought about products such as toothpaste (invented in 3000 BC), eyeglasses (262 AD), flushable toilets (the sixteenth century), clothes dryers (early nineteenth century), can openers (1813), fax machines (1843—that's right, invented in 1843!), credit cards (1920s), sliced bread (1928), computer mouses (1964), Post-It notes (1980), and DVDs (1995).

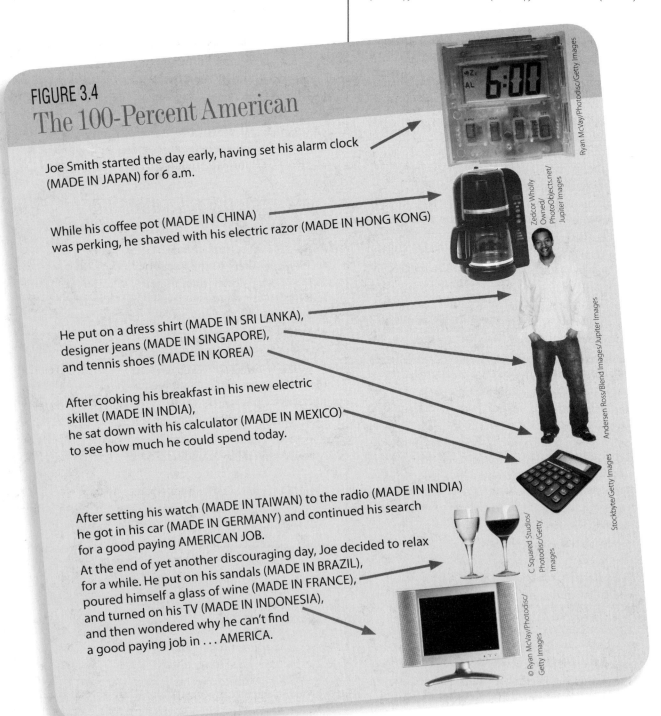

FIGURE 3.4
The 100-Percent American

Joe Smith started the day early, having set his alarm clock (MADE IN JAPAN) for 6 a.m.

While his coffee pot (MADE IN CHINA) was perking, he shaved with his electric razor (MADE IN HONG KONG)

He put on a dress shirt (MADE IN SRI LANKA), designer jeans (MADE IN SINGAPORE), and tennis shoes (MADE IN KOREA)

After cooking his breakfast in his new electric skillet (MADE IN INDIA), he sat down with his calculator (MADE IN MEXICO) to see how much he could spend today.

After setting his watch (MADE IN TAIWAN) to the radio (MADE IN INDIA) he got in his car (MADE IN GERMANY) and continued his search for a good paying AMERICAN JOB.

At the end of yet another discouraging day, Joe decided to relax for a while. He put on his sandals (MADE IN BRAZIL), poured himself a glass of wine (MADE IN FRANCE), and turned on his TV (MADE IN INDONESIA), and then wondered why he can't find a good paying job in . . . AMERICA.

Ryan McVay/Photodisc/Getty Images

Zedcor Wholly Owned/PhotoObjects.net/Jupiter Images

Andersen Ross/Blend Images/Jupiter Images

Stockbyte/Getty Images

C Squared Studios/Photodisc/Getty Images

© Ryan McVay/Photodisc/Getty Images

Innovation—turning inventions into mass-market products—also sparks cultural changes. An innovator is someone determined to market an invention, even if it's someone else's good idea. For example, Henry Ford invented nothing new but "assembled into a car the discoveries of other men behind whom were centuries of work," an innovation that changed people's lives (Evans et al. 2006: 465).

Discovery

Like invention, *discovery* requires exploration and investigation and results in new products, insights, ideas, or behavior. The discovery of penicillin prolonged lives, which, in turn, meant that more grandparents (as well as great-grandparents) and grandchildren would get to know each other. However, longer lifespans also mean that children and grandchildren need to care for elderly family members over many years (see Chapter 13).

Discovery usually requires dedicated work and years of commitment, but some discoveries occur by chance. This is called the *serendipity effect*. For example, George de Mestral, a Swiss electrical engineer, was hiking through the woods. He was annoyed by burrs that clung to his clothing. Why were they so difficult to remove? A closer examination showed that the burrs had hook-like arms that locked into the open weave of his clothes. The discovery led de Mestral to invent a hook-and-loop fastener. His invention, Velcro—derived from the French words *velour* (velvet) and *crochet* (hooks)—can be now found on everything from clothing to spacecraft.

External Pressures

External pressure for cultural change can take various forms. In its most direct form—war, conquest, or colonization—the dominant group uses force or the threat of force to bring about cultural change in the other group. When the Soviet Union invaded and took over many small countries (such as Lithuania, Latvia, Estonia, Ukraine, Georgia, and Armenia) after World War II, it forbade citizens to speak their native languages, banned traditions and customs, and turned churches into warehouses.

Pressures for change can also be indirect. For example, some countries—such as Thailand, Vietnam, China, and Russia—have reduced their prostitution and international sex trafficking because of widespread criticism by the United Nations and some European countries (but not the United States). The United Nations has no power to intervene in a country's internal affairs but can embarrass nations by publicizing human rights violations (Farley 2001).

> **cultural lag** the gap when nonmaterial culture changes more slowly than material culture.

Changes in the Physical Environment

Changes in the physical environment also lead to cultural change. The potato blight in Ireland during the 1840s spurred massive emigration to the United States. Natural disasters, like earthquakes and floods, may cause death, destruction of homes, and other devastation. People may suffer depression because of the immense losses they have experienced (see Chapters 13 and 14). Disasters may also bring positive change. After major earthquakes in California, for instance, studies of architectural design resulted in new building codes that protected businesses and residences from collapsing during minor earthquakes (Bohannon 2005).

TECHNOLOGY AND CULTURAL LAG

Some parts of culture change more rapidly than others. **Cultural lag** refers to the gap when nonmaterial culture changes more slowly than material culture.

There are numerous examples of cultural lag in modern society, because ethical rules and government regulations haven't kept up with technological developments. Recently, for example, a graduate student posted a paper on a university Web site and found out, later, that an Internet term-paper mill was selling it without her knowledge or permission. Because intellectual property laws applying to Internet use are still being developed, this student was in court for several years before the Web site operator settled for an undisclosed amount (Foster 2006).

Cultural lag often creates uncertainty, ambiguity about what's right and wrong, conflicting values, and a feeling of helplessness. According to Naisbitt and his colleagues (1999: 3), we live in a "technologically intoxicated zone" where we both fear and worship technology, become obsessed with gadgets (like computers) even though they take up much of our time, don't deal with ethical issues raised by biotechnology (like the implications of cloning embryos), and rely on technology as quick fixes: "We want to believe that any given solution is only a purchase away."

Cultural lags have always existed and will continue in the future. Technology is necessary, but we can make conscious choices about how and when we use technological advances. Thus, cultural lags can be